An Aviator's Field Guide to
Owning an Airplane

An Aviator's Field Guide to
Owning an Airplane
Practical insights for successful
aircraft ownership

Jason Blair

AVIATION SUPPLIES & ACADEMICS
NEWCASTLE, WASHINGTON

An Aviator's Field Guide to Owning an Airplane:
Practical insights for successful aircraft ownership
by Jason Blair

Aviation Supplies & Academics, Inc.
7005 132nd Place SE
Newcastle, Washington 98059-3153
asa@asa2fly.com | www.asa2fly.com

See ASA's website at www.asa2fly.com/reader/avown for the "Reader Resources" page containing additional information and updates relating to this book.

None of the material in this book supersedes any operational documents or procedures issued by the Federal Aviation Administration or other governing agency, manufacturers, schools, or operator standard operating procedures.

ASA-AVOWN
ISBN 978-1-61954-845-9

Additional formats available:
Kindle   ISBN 978-1-61954-847-3
eBook ePub   ISBN 978-1-61954-846-6
eBook PDF   ISBN 978-1-61954-848-0

Printed in the United States of America.
2024   2023   2022   2021   2020   9 8 7 6 5 4 3 2 1
Cover photo: Greg Brown

Library of Congress Cataloging-in-Publication Data
Names: Blair, Jason, author.
Title: An aviator's field guide to owning an airplane : practical insights for successful aircraft
    ownership / Jason Blair.
Description: Newcastle, Washington : Aviation Supplies & Academics, Inc., [2020]
Identifiers: LCCN 2019017831| ISBN 9781619548480 (trade pbk. : alk. paper) | ISBN
    1619548488 (trade pbk. : alk. paper)
Subjects: LCSH: Private planes—Purchasing. | Airplanes—Ownership. | Private planes—
    Maintenance and repair. | Private planes—Cost of operation.
Classification: LCC TL671.85 .B533 2020 | DDC 629.133/34029—dc23
LC record available at https://lccn.loc.gov/2019017831

Contents

Acknowledgments

A special thanks is due to Charles Warren, a good friend who isn't a pilot but is a fellow writer from another industry. He spent a significant amount of time helping review the content of this book. His help was instrumental in getting the content of this book from the first draft to the final draft that was submitted to ASA for its amazing staff to refine into this final product. An author is only a part of the process that makes books like this possible for readers.

I would also be remiss if I didn't thank my dear wife, Aimee. This is the fourth book I have written in two years, and without her help and some pre-editing on her part, much of this content would not have been possible. It is a special thing when your spouse can be the biggest part of your team. Her help and support have been a source of major assistance and a motivator through all of my work and life.

Introduction

So you just bought an aircraft, or perhaps you have owned one for a while. In either case, this doesn't mean you know everything there is to know about owning an aircraft, maintaining it, and what you can do with it! Although I don't know everything either, I do have a great deal of experience and knowledge gained from years of aircraft ownership and helping advise clients and friends through their purchases and ownership of aircraft. I hope that by sharing what I've learned, it may help you discover a few new tricks or avoid pitfalls that I—and my customers—have experienced over the years. We all can learn from our mistakes and those of others!

Aircraft ownership certainly comes with benefits. It allows an operator to travel and to see the world in a way that goes beyond the experiences of others who are limited by being bound by gravity to the Earth's surface. Even people who travel via commercial aviation or who rent aircraft periodically find themselves more limited than those of us who own aircraft and can use them at will.

Aircraft owners may think about travel in a different way than the majority of the population. Owners are not encumbered by the thoughts of long travel requirements to get to faraway locations. Considerations of how early to arrive at the airport ahead of time to accommodate for check-in or security checkpoint inspections are things of the past. And because of the large number of airports that can be used, aircraft ownership vastly increases the locations to which an owner may travel in relatively quick periods of time. Aircraft become machines of time travel reduction, business tools, or just ways to enjoy looking down at the earth on a sunny Saturday.

The joys of aircraft ownership stem from their utility and the fact that they let us do something our natural bodies were never intended to do. We can defy the restrictions of gravity and expedite travel times by going more directly and quickly than is possible with other modes of transportation.

However, with these joys come responsibilities, expenses, and challenges that owners must address to keep making these benefits possible. Ownership requires the consideration of maintenance requirements, fixed and relative costs, management of documentary requirements, and planning for future needs of the aircraft. These considerations and the challenges they present go well beyond what most pilots are taught during their initial, or even advanced, flight training activities. The reason is that most pilots are taught to be pilots, not owners. There is a difference.

A good owner knows how to properly manage an aircraft to keep it safe and in service. An aircraft that is not able to be flown is of no good to its owner. It just becomes an expense without providing any of the benefits that should come with ownership.

Whether you are a first-time owner or someone who has owned a few aircraft previously, there most likely is information that can help you be a better owner but that no one has ever shared with you. An aircraft is a big investment. I want you to get the most out of your aircraft, protect and maintain it to the best of your ability, and enjoy the utility it provides.

The content in this book is not intended to make you a better pilot. It is intended to make you a better owner.

Now that I have provided this short introduction, let's move on to discuss the many topics that can make your aircraft ownership experience the best possible.

Chapter 1

The Real Cost of Ownership

The initial purchase cost is not the only cost associated with owning an aircraft. While most owners understand this before they purchase an aircraft, not all owners really calculate the full costs associated with ownership. Some of these costs are easy to overlook and exclude in personal or business budget considerations, but it is worth it for owners to take the time to fully evaluate what the financial footprint of aircraft ownership really will be.

Hopefully you did some of this evaluation before you chose to purchase an aircraft, and perhaps you are an old hat at this. But if not, some of the considerations in this chapter will help you better understand the real costs of owning an aircraft.

Let's start by breaking down the costs of aircraft ownership into three major categories. These are:

- Fixed costs
- Variable costs
- Unexpected costs

The fixed costs include costs that will not change based on how much you use the aircraft. They are expenses that occur whether you fly 300 hours in a year or don't fly the aircraft even one hour. These include costs such as hangar rent or utilities, annual registration fees, insurance on the aircraft, and to some degree, the annual inspection.

Variable costs include the fuel used on a per-hour basis, the number of oil changes that will be completed, perhaps some level of reserve for various future expenses such as engine or propeller overhauls, and any other periodic costs that are encountered based on actual usage hours of the aircraft.

Unexpected costs are the hardest to account for in an aircraft operating budget. For our purposes here, we will assume that the aircraft keeps running properly with a normal course of maintenance, but it is worth considering some amount of additional operating reserves since components do break on aircraft over time.

With that in mind, let's actually go through the effort of considering what a typical general aviation aircraft may cost an owner per year and per hour of operation.

First, in order to really figure out how much an aircraft costs to operate, we also have to realistically consider how many hours it will be flown per year. While many owners fly their aircraft much less, let's assume for demonstration purposes that the owner will fly the aircraft 150 hours per year. With that baseline established, we can compare yearly hours of usage with all the expected costs in order to establish an hourly equivalent cost of operation.

We will also assume that the owner completes an oil change every 50 hours (Figure 1).

Yearly Expected Operation and Oil Changes		Description
Yearly expected operation	150 hours	The expected yearly hours that will be flown.
Oil change increment	50 hours	The expected hours between oil changes.
Number of oil changes per year	3	

Figure 1. Expected yearly hours of operation and number of oil changes.

We will then assume we know the fixed costs associated with the aircraft, such as the yearly insurance costs, the monthly hangar cost, and a base annual inspection cost typical for this aircraft.

By doing this, we can come up with a calculation of what these costs will add up to on a yearly basis, and then divide this total by how many hours the owner has used the aircraft.

This calculation provides an hourly fixed cost of operation for the aircraft based on expected usage throughout one year of operation. This can be seen in Figure 2.

Fixed Costs			
	Monthly	Yearly	Description
Storage cost	$200	$2,400	Monthly expected hangar, tie-down, or storage rent or cost.
Hangar utilities	$40	$480	Monthly expected hangar, tie-down, or storage utilities expenses.
Insurance		$1,200	Yearly insurance cost.
Annual inspection		$3,000	Expected cost of an annual inspection for the aircraft.
Total fixed costs per year		$7,080	The total of fixed costs per year for the aircraft.
Per-hour fixed cost		**$47.20**	The resulting per-hour fixed cost contribution to operation that would be required based on the number of hours flown per year (150).

Figure 2. Calculation of fixed cost of operation per hour.

This is significant as we consider the fact that over the expected 150 hours of operation, fixed costs equate to less than $50 per hour of operation but total $7,080 throughout the year. Since these costs are fixed, this means that even if the owner did not actually fly the aircraft the expected 150 hours, or in fact didn't fly it at all during the year, the same $7,080 cost would still be incurred!

Let's move on to consider variable costs that will be incurred as the owner uses the aircraft. Variable costs are those that change in direct relation to operation of the aircraft; the variable cost per hour of operation is constant, but as the aircraft is flown more hours, total variable costs will increase.

Returning to the oil change increments from Figure 1, the expected 150 hours of flight per year, and assuming a reasonable cost of $150 per oil change, we find that this will add an additional $3.00 per hour for operational costs. These calculations are shown in Figure 3.

Oil Change Cost Calculation		Description
Oil change cost	$150	The expected cost of an oil/filter change, including labor and parts.
Number of oil changes per year	3	This is based on the hours of use expected and the desired oil change interval (Figure 1).
Expected oil change expenses per year	$450	The total yearly cost of oil changes.
Hourly cost of oil changes	**$3.00**	The expected hourly cost of oil changes (based on 150 hours of operation per year).

Figure 3. Calculation of hourly cost of oil changes.

Other variable costs include reserve costs, which I encourage all owners to consider—and even actually put funds aside for—as they operate their aircraft. This will allow an owner to plan for major maintenance items such as engine overhauls, propeller overhauls, or avionics maintenance or upgrades. The vast majority of owners don't actually put this money aside in a bank account, although it's a good idea to do so, but they should at least consider reserve costs as part of the real operating cost of the aircraft.

If we start by considering an engine reserve, we would look at the current time on the engine, when the manufacturer recommends that the engine be overhauled, and how much such an overhaul typically costs.

The example in Figure 4 shows a conservative estimate of an aircraft that has 800 hours already on an engine, a 2,000-hour manufacturer's recommended overhaul period, and an expected $25,000 overhaul cost (including removing the engine and reinstalling it after the overhaul). These calculations reveal that this aircraft should be budgeting $20.83 per flight hour toward an engine overhaul.

Engine Reserve Calculation*		Description
Current engine time (SMOH)	800 hours	The current engine tach time (SMOH = since major overhaul).
Time between overhauls (TBO)	2,000 hours	The manufacturer's recommended TBO hours for the engine, or a time that you expect it will need to be completed.
Flight time to engine overhaul	1,200 hours	The expected remaining hours able to be flown until an engine overhaul is required.
Estimated engine overhaul cost	$25,000	The expected cost of an overhaul or replacement of the engine, including the engine and all labor.
Engine hourly reserve required	**$20.83**	The hourly reserve required to be saved to allow the engine to be overhauled or replaced when due under normal conditions.

*For one engine, assuming a single-engine aircraft.

Figure 4. Calculation of per-hour cost for engine reserve.

This represents a significant hourly cost for the aircraft. If we assume that the aircraft engine is approximately midway through its manufacturer's recommended life, we have to amortize the cost of an engine overhaul across the time left until the recommended overhaul.

In fact, the engine may be OK to operate a little longer, or perhaps it won't last as long as expected, but this is about as good of an estimate as we can make without having a crystal ball to know if anything will fail earlier or if the engine will be airworthy well beyond the manufacturer's recommended times.

On any aircraft that has a propeller that requires overhaul, the same calculation should be made. Assuming the propeller has the same SMOH and TBO times as the engine (it is common that propellers and engines are overhauled at the same time), we can calculate how much on an hourly basis an owner should allocate toward a propeller reserve. This is shown in Figure 5, assuming the propeller overhaul will cost the owner $5,000 when it is completed.

Propeller Reserve Calculation*		Description
Current propeller time (SMOH)	800 hours	The current propeller tach time.
Time between overhauls (TBO)	2,000 hours	The manufacturer's recommended TBO hours for the propeller, or the time interval that you expect it will need to be completed.
Flight time to propeller overhaul	1,200 hours	The expected remaining hours able to be flown until a propeller overhaul is required.
Estimated propeller overhaul cost	$5,000	The expected cost of an overhaul or replacement of the propeller, including the propeller and all labor.
Propeller hourly reserve required	**$4.17**	The hourly reserve required to be saved to allow the propeller to be overhauled or replaced when due under normal conditions.

*For one propeller. For aircraft with multiple propellers, increase required reserve proportionately.

Figure 5. Calculation of per-hour cost for propeller reserve.

This might seem like a small number, but an additional $4.17 toward the operating cost per hour does add up over the course of a year.

It's also a good plan to consider and include general reserve costs to be used for the airframe, any avionics work, or a broader general category. These may include expenses for things such as changing tires or a dented flap that happens from a little hangar rash.

If we plan a conservative $5.00 per hour for each of these categories, this will add an additional $15.00 per hour of operation for all these additional reserve costs (Figure 6). This can help an owner account for unexpected maintenance costs that may arise during the life of the aircraft.

General Reserve Costs to Allocate		Description
Airframe	$5.00	The expected general airframe reserve per hour of flight to accommodate for any airframe maintenance beyond the cost of annual inspections.
Avionics	$5.00	The expected general avionics reserve per hour of flight to cover repair or replacement of items due to wear and tear.
General	$5.00	The expected general overall aircraft reserve per hour of flight to accommodate for maintenance outside typical annual inspection wear and tear costs. This could include potential breakage or other damage.
Total per-hour allocation for general reserve	**$15.00**	

Figure 6. Calculation of general reserve costs to allocate per hour of operation.

And at this point, we still have not accounted for any fuel usage! If we assume the aircraft uses 10 gallons per hour in operation at a cost of $4.50 per gallon, then we will spend an additional $45.00 per hour just on fuel (Figure 7).

Expected Fuel Burn and Costs		Description
Gallons used per hour	10	The number of gallons of fuel the aircraft burns per hour in normal operations (total for all engines).
Fuel price per gallon	$4.50	The expected average cost of fuel per gallon.
Total fuel cost per hour	**$45.00**	The cost of fuel per hour of operation, considered in wet rate evaluation of the aircraft.

Figure 7. Calculation of estimated cost of fuel per hour of operation.

Totaling all of these costs results in an hourly operating cost that will surprise most owners.

With the basic variable and fixed costs accounted for across an estimated 150 hours of yearly use, we can find the operating costs in both dry and wet (fuel included) conditions on an hourly basis (Figure 8).

Cost per Hour of Operations		Description
Fixed Costs	$47.20	Costs of storage, hangar utilities, insurance, annual inspection (Figure 2).
Oil changes	$3.00	(Calculated in Figure 3.)
Engine reserve	$20.83	(Calculated in Figure 4.)
Propeller reserve	$4.17	(Calculated in Figure 5.)
General reserve	$15.00	(Calculated in Figure 6.)
Total hourly cost of operation (Dry)	**$90.20**	The amount the aircraft is costing per hour of operation including all above costs but without consideration of fuel costs.
Fuel cost	$45.00	(Calculated in Figure 7.)
Total hourly cost of operation (Wet)	**$135.20**	The cost per hour of aircraft operation including fuel costs.

Figure 8. Total operating costs per hour (dry and wet).

What is even more telling—and in some ways, scary—is to consider what the total *yearly* operating cost is, not just what the hourly cost is to operate. If an owner uses an aircraft for 150 hours per year (such as in this example), the real cost of ownership and operation will be as shown in Figure 9.

Yearly Operating Costs (based on expected 150 hours per year of use)		Description
Total expense of operation per year (dry) ($90.20/hour × 150 hours)	$13,530	The total expense an owner would incur based on the expected 150 hours of operation per year. This represents the total cost including reserves the aircraft will realistically experience, without consideration of fuel costs.
Total expense of operation per year (wet) ($135.20/hour × 150 hours)	$20,280	Total real expenses including fuel on a yearly basis. This represents the real "out-of-pocket total" that would be experienced.

Figure 9. Total yearly cost of ownership (based on 150 hours of operation).

When you look at the cost of an aircraft by considering the total yearly expense, it may seem like a much bigger number than what you might assume if you only consider the costs of flying on weekends and filling up the gas tanks!

However, it is important for owners to consider this yearly total because it is their real cost of ownership. Without calculating the costs as we've just done above, many owners will end up spending much more money on a yearly basis than they originally expected to. Chapter 19 provides another example showing calculations for a different aircraft and also goes into more detail about planning and budgeting costs for future maintenance or upgrades that you might want to consider incorporating into your yearly total.

Adding up these expenses helps an owner really understand if the total yearly cost of operating an aircraft is within their budget. If you don't think you can spend at least $20,000 each year without it negatively affecting more important budget items in your life, perhaps it is time to consider not being an aircraft owner. This can be a hard choice to make, but many owners have found themselves in the position where they are unable to support the expensive footprint of aircraft ownership. This situation commonly results in the aircraft falling into disrepair as it sits in a hangar.

It's worth noting that as you use an aircraft more, the fixed costs become spread over a greater number of hours of operation. This will actually decrease the hourly fixed operating cost of the aircraft. However, the variable costs are spread equally, as by definition they are incurred per hour of flight. This means that although the total *hourly* operating cost may decrease (because of the lower per-hour fixed cost), the total *yearly* operating cost will still increase as more hours are flown because the total variable operations costs increase proportionately to the number of hours flown. Flying more hours also means you will need to allocate more "reserve" costs each year than if you flew fewer hours and were able to spread those costs over more years.

It is all a trade-off to some degree, but by taking the time to do the math, you will be able to fully understand what your real costs of aircraft ownership are based on your fixed and variable expenses. This can allow you to accurately track your expenses to determine if the costs of operating a specific aircraft are in line with the budget that you need to operate within. If the costs do not match your budget, it may be time to switch aircraft or even consider no longer being an aircraft owner.

Do you want to get a better idea of what it really costs to own a specific aircraft? To assist in this process, I created a basic personal aircraft operating cost calculator that you can use to track some of the more common costs and get a better idea of what your real cost of ownership is. (See the online Reader Resources at www.asa2fly. com/reader/avown.) If you have never thoroughly calculated all the costs associated with aircraft ownership, it may surprise you how high the actual costs are per year or per hour of flight operation.

Chapter 2

Using Your Aircraft

Although this is the second chapter in this book, it was the last chapter I wrote. In some senses, it was the hardest one for me to write. I have seen many aircraft owners stop using their aircraft, known many aspiring buyers who had dreams of all the ways they would use an aircraft, and encountered so many in-betweens that it is hard to give advice to people on how to use their aircraft. I think the best advice I can give is the simplest: If you have an aircraft, just use it. Somehow.

I won't presume to tell you how you should use your aircraft. To some degree that is a personal choice—it depends on the type of aircraft and what it can be used for; it depends on family dynamics; and it depends on whether you bought it as a traveling tool or as a fun machine for some stress relief. In short, it depends on many factors. With that said, what I will tell you is to use your aircraft.

The worst thing you can do with your aircraft is not use it. A sitting airplane often will have more things go wrong with it than one that is actively used. And, if you already own an aircraft, you are already paying for the fixed costs associated with it. Use the darn thing!

I encourage owners to keep their aircraft actively operating. Normally I recommend that an aircraft be operated at least once every two weeks, and I tell most owners to aim for a minimum of at least 100 hours of operation per year. This keeps the aircraft fluids moving, seals lubricated, and moving components, well, moving. In an aircraft at rest over long periods, these things begin to degrade. The longer an aircraft sits unused, the more of these items that will dry out, freeze up, and become more prone to breaking. I know it may sound counterintuitive that using an aircraft less will make it more likely that parts will break, but I have experienced this in many cases to some degree.

Owners use their aircraft for any number of things ranging from taking local flights around the area to taking trips for business, flying their families on long vacations each summer, or even challenging themselves to compete in aerobatics if they have the right kind of airplane and training. What you use your aircraft for is highly dependent on the aircraft you have chosen to own, your aviation goals, and perhaps even the phase of your life. Some aircraft owners may transition between multiple aircraft during their lives.

One friend of mine started his aircraft ownership with a Cessna 172, and as his business grew, he progressed to a Beechcraft Baron and then ended up with a Piper Meridian that helped him travel for business. As he aged and eventually retired, the Meridian wasn't really needed anymore, so he downsized back to a Baron for him and his wife to use for travel and added a Cessna 182 on floats for fun flight and fishing trips. His own desires for using his aircraft changed over time and, as a result, so did the aircraft he owned.

Another friend had a Piper Seneca for years until his kids grew up and went off to college. At that point he found that it was only him and his wife who were still traveling on the aircraft, so he ended up with a Van's RV-6 for quicker and more efficient travel.

Yet another friend has a wife who doesn't enjoy flying, so he bought a Pitts S1. It's a single-seat aerobatic aircraft that he flies just for fun to challenge his skill set as he practices aerobatics.

Each of these examples shows varied aircraft used for different purposes. And that's the way it should be. As an owner, it is your choice what you want to do with your aircraft. However, I think it is important to also understand what your aircraft cannot do.

If you are planning the trip of a lifetime and taking along 300 pounds of luggage and the kitchen sink, your Cessna 150 may not be the plane to get it done. But if that is not your typical use for the aircraft, it doesn't mean you have to sell your Cessna 150 and buy a bigger airplane. You could always rent an aircraft for that one-time trip. There may not be one aircraft that will be right for or capable of every type of flight you want to take, but it makes sense to own an aircraft that works well for the majority of your usage. Just be realistic with yourself about what you plan to do with your aircraft.

Are you planning on using your aircraft for business travel? Many people do this. If you intend to, I recommend that you plan accordingly and perhaps have backup plans in case of delays due to aircraft maintenance needs or weather, and you should be prepared for some instances in which you may not be able to use the aircraft at all.

Whether you own your own business or work for another company, using your aircraft for business trips can expedite travel, saving travel time by getting you to more places and/or back home more quickly. Aircraft can really be time-saving machines when used properly. With that said, not every company allows owners to fly their own aircraft for work travel. Ask ahead about limitations and plan appropriately.

In some cases, flying your aircraft for business purposes may provide surprises. One friend worked for a company that not only paid his fuel bills when he used his aircraft for business travel but was also willing to reimburse him a specified rate per hour of flight toward his maintenance costs! An owner in such a situation should discuss this with an accountant to ensure it is handled properly. In the above case, the owner was an accountant, so it was easy for him to set it up himself.

For three years, I used a Piper Cherokee as my commuting vehicle to work. I lived in the lower peninsula of Michigan and worked in Oshkosh, Wisconsin. It's about a 6½ hour drive between the two, but it was only a 1½ hour flight. I would fly to work on Monday and return home on Thursday or Friday, dependent on weather, of course. I calculated that this saved me a little more than *17 full days* of time per year! That was one heck of a savings in commuting time, and it certainly was more enjoyable than driving through Chicago traffic twice a week. I know that not everyone will be able to justify this for their daily commute, but it certainly may be an option for a few owners.

Many owners buy an aircraft to train in. Maybe it is for an initial pilot certificate, or perhaps to add an instrument rating, or even to build time and not have to pay rental charges as they work toward certificates and ratings to make them employable at airlines. I honestly think this is an underutilized option when it comes to aircraft ownership. Especially for savvy owners who condense the footprint of their training and minimize ownership costs over a short period of time before selling the aircraft, purchasing an aircraft to use for training can actually reduce the overall training cost and lend some consistency to the aircraft the pilot uses during training. If you are going to train in your aircraft, take the time to make sure that the instructor you choose is familiar with and proficient in the make and model of aircraft. Your insurance may require it, and your training will be better.

At a minimum, make sure you get some recurrent training in your aircraft periodically. It is easy to get into a rut with your normal operations and not get the opportunity to stretch your skills in your aircraft. Many owners can't remember the last time they practiced stalls in their aircraft, yet stall/spin accidents are still one of the biggest loss of control accidents that owners experience. Have a good instructor go with you occasionally, and work on stretching those skills or adding some new ones to keep your skills sharp and expanding.

If you will not personally be using your aircraft a significant amount of time each year, you may want to consider sharing it or finding ways it can generate some revenue to help alleviate the costs of ownership. I'll tell you honestly that it may not always, or even regularly, result in a profit, but it can help defray some costs.

This does not mean you have to turn your brand-new Cirrus SR22T over to the local flight school for primary training and get it beat up, but you might consider leasing it to a local company or a charter operator. The type of aircraft you have and the other operations based at your airport or nearby will be factors in these decisions. Any aircraft that is operated by others besides the owner will be subject to some additional wear and tear, but it may be a fact you are willing to live with if the benefits are worth it.

An aircraft that is used commercially (i.e., one that is generating income based on the aircraft use) will typically be subject to some additional maintenance requirements. If it is on a "charter certificate" or used in "flight training," it generally will require 100-hour inspections that will happen between annual inspections. Be aware of any additional maintenance requirements that will be caused by commercial activity and carefully consider if these extra costs will be greater or less than the revenue generated. That can be a deciding factor in whether you choose to use your aircraft in some commercial capacity.

Another option may be to establish or put your aircraft into an existing club or shared ownership access option. If you don't use your aircraft extensively, there might be another friend or partner you could consider who might be interested in using the aircraft. This isn't necessarily a commercial activity, but it could be a shared operating relationship that helps not only keep the aircraft operating but pay for the costs. Many great aviation friendships over the years have been established by sharing an aircraft. However, a word of warning that many friendships have also been broken by shared ownership of an aircraft.

If I am going to give one piece of advice for any owner thinking about leasing, sharing, establishing a club, or renting their aircraft to others, it is this: Plan from the beginning of any such relationship to establish how it will be ended and have that clearly drawn up in a written agreement.

While any relationship can go sour, they often deteriorate more quickly when there are different expectations among the parties about how the relationship will be terminated. You can avoid that situation by making sure before starting any business or shared operating or ownership relationship that you have clear operating documents or contracts that can be referenced if one (or more) of the parties wants out, wants their money back, or wants to sell the aircraft.

There are numerous ways you can use your aircraft, and I hope that you will find ways to do so for many years to come. As you do, I also hope that the information in this book will help make that ownership more successful and affordable as well as make your operation safer. On that note, I just want to reiterate several important points about using your aircraft.

Use your aircraft, stay current, and more importantly stay proficient for the type of flying you are going to do. If you are not proficient, be honest with yourself and don't fly until you take the time to get proficient or get some instruction. Ensuring you maintain your proficiency will have a positive effect on the safety of your flight operations.

Many of the FAA Aviation Safety Inspectors (ASIs) I talk with tell me that incidents and accidents involving general aviation aircraft owners and pilots occur more commonly at certain times of the year. These accidents and incidents often coincide with holidays such as Memorial Day, the Fourth of July, and Labor Day or with periods such as spring break. These are times that owners may have off from work or other commitments but perhaps when they have not had enough other time off recently to fly and stay proficient; now they have committed themselves to flying a family trip or other outing and feel the pressure of "get-there-itis." In such a situation, they may make questionable decisions about the crosswinds in which they fly or the IFR conditions they are legal but not proficient to fly in, or they may stretch that fuel range a little further than the tanks really allow. Sometimes these decisions result in catastrophic results.

Legal currency is, as all pilots know, different than actual proficiency for a given flight operation. One of the benefits of owning an aircraft is the ability to fly for more than just legal currency, but actually having access to an aircraft to fly for true proficiency. Owning an aircraft provides you with the opportunity to fly more frequently than perhaps would be possible if you were renting, but it takes dedication to stay proficient so that when those special weekend trips are upon you, you are comfortable and capable of making the flights safely. This is just another good reason to get out there and fly that aircraft you own. See, it's OK to tell your husband or wife that you really *need* to go fly some more. It's a safety thing—or it's at least a good excuse.

Chapter 3

Insuring Your Aircraft

Aircraft insurance may seem expensive and can be confusing for many people. It is something you hope you will never need, but you really want to have it in case you do. You can't buy insurance to cover a problem after it has already occurred. And it's almost worse to discover after a problem arises that you picked the wrong agent, brokerage, or coverage. With that said, unlike the insurance requirements for ground-based passenger vehicles such as your family car, insurance is not actually required to be maintained on an FAA-registered aircraft. Isn't that crazy?

The basic reason for this is that aircraft are federally registered vehicles, and vehicle insurance is administered by state insurance regulations. Because of this discrepancy, in short, insurance cannot be mandated by state-administered insurance practices on federally registered vehicles. So, until something in that relationship changes, insurance on aircraft is technically optional—at least from a government standpoint.

However, insurance is regularly required to be in place when a loan is given for an aircraft purchase. It may also be required by hangar rental agreements, airport operating guidelines, or other similar, more localized, situational conditions. For these reasons as well as obvious asset and liability protection, most owners do choose to insure their aircraft.

Choosing the Insured Value

For aircraft insurance, the value that is assigned to the aircraft is determined by the owner and set in the individual's insurance policy. This is different than the more familiar insurance market for passenger cars in which the value of a personal car is usually established based on an industry "blue-book" value if the vehicle is damaged. But for aircraft, the value is designated by the owner and an insurance policy premium is determined based on that value.

This means, for example, that if an owner totals his Cessna 172 in an accident and has set its value as $100,000, but a similar replacement could potentially be purchased on the used market for only $75,000, the insurance company will still write a check for the full insured value of $100,000. This is a good thing should owners find themselves in need of this payout! Hopefully you never find yourself in this situation, but if you do, your payout will not be reduced—it will be based on the value you set and have been paying a premium on all along.

Considering this, many owners choose to keep the insured value of their aircraft a little higher than the purchase price they paid. This allows them to ensure they will be fully covered in the event of a problem. If you do this, however, keep in mind that you will be paying the premium based on this higher value. If you want to reduce your insurance premium, stating a lower hull value can help, but it also means that your payout may be lower than a replacement cost if it ever comes to that. This decision may depend a bit on how much of a gamble you want to take, and you have to determine what will work best for your situation. This is also worth discussing with your insurance agent.

In addition, it is also important to understand that "hull" insurance is different than "liability" or "medical" coverage, and these can be selected at different values. With that in mind, let's look at the differences.

Hull Coverage

Hull coverage is the coverage in place that you will get for the replacement value or "fix-it" costs for any damage to the actual physical aircraft that you are going to operate.

As I noted previously, this insured value is designated by the owner/operator. They may set that value based on the expected replacement value or, when required, what loan value needs to be covered.

The two major categories to consider when purchasing hull coverage relate to "in-motion" or "not-in-motion" coverage. For an aircraft that is being operated (as we hope they all are), "in-motion" coverage is what will cover the aircraft when it is flown. However, an owner may choose to only purchase "not-in-motion" coverage, which would only cover the aircraft when it is not being flown and is typically available at a much lower premium cost. This provides coverage for non-flying damage, such as a flood or hangar roof collapse. Not-in-motion coverage can be a good option for some owners, such as those who are restoring an aircraft or perhaps have parked their aircraft while working on getting their medical back after an issue.

Liability and/or Medical Coverage

Liability coverage and medical coverage are intended to cover damage done by an aircraft or operator to other persons or property. These are the costs that can really skyrocket quickly if an accident takes place.

Property liability coverage will cover any damage to other aircraft, houses, roads, farmland, or anything else you happen to land on, crash into, or damage in the process of generating any insurance claim. Property liability coverage typically has a much higher limit than the hull value of the aircraft, and an underwriter may offer different levels for different prices. An owner's choice of what level to choose and how much risk to take is a somewhat personal decision, but it can affect the total policy values and cost per year.

Individual or occupant liability coverage is commonly included in this area of coverage. Without sounding too morbid or insensitive, this is basically a value maximum set for each person who could be killed in an accident. It is worth noting what these maximums are because people are the most expensive (most "valuable") part of what is covered by insurance. An underwriter would probably happily prefer to write a check any day to replace an aircraft rather than make a payout for a death in an accident—from a purely business point of view, not to mention the obvious human tragedy involved in such a loss.

A policy will also often include coverage for medical expenses. While occupants may have personal health insurance, in a vehicle accident the coverage from the policy covering the vehicle operation will typically be the first to be applied.

These are the three major components of the liability coverage—property, individual/occupant, and medical expense liability coverage—that many pilots select for their aircraft. For each, it is worth evaluating what level of coverage is best for your situation and deciding whether you want the coverage to be a "smooth" value (meaning a maximum total) or to be set on a "per occupant" or "per occurrence" basis.

Some owners choose to purchase liability insurance without also purchasing hull coverage. This offers coverage for operations but not necessarily the vehicle asset itself. While this approach can reduce rates, it also comes with the obvious financial risk of having to personally cover the cost to fix or replace your aircraft if it is damaged.

Spend time with your agent to find the best mix of these coverage alternatives to meet your particular needs. It is worth taking the time to fully understand your insurance coverage options and what these options will cover—and what they won't.

Add-Ons for Insurance

Having only the basic coverage may not be all that you want or need. There may be additional coverage options that you were not even aware of—so be sure to ask your agent what is available.

Owners will often find that for a minimal extra cost, they can add on "non-owned" coverage. This is coverage that will give you some level of protection if you borrow a friend's airplane or rent one from the local FBO. The limits may be different than those in your primary aircraft policy, but this added coverage can be great to have if you plan to fly aircraft other than your own.

Legal and certificate action coverage can also commonly be added to policies at a very affordable rate. This will kick in to provide coverage for legal services fees to defend your pilot certificate in the event of any FAA enforcement action. This coverage will also offer support for fees associated with defending any liability litigation for damage in an accident or for other similar expenses. This can be the most valuable part of the liability side of the insurance equation. In many instances, the legal expenses associated with an accident far exceed any physical, medical, or property damage costs. This coverage can be the make-or-break factor in a pilot's personal financial future.

Know the Policy Limitations

I know those insurance contracts are long, but you really should read them and make sure you understand your policy's limitations to ensure that if you do need the coverage, it will be applicable.

For example, if you are planning that trip of a lifetime to the North Pole, make sure your policy doesn't exempt coverage north of 60 degrees latitude (many do). If you are heading off to the Bahamas, make sure your policy is not limited to just the continental United States. Are you planning to fly the North Atlantic over to Europe? You will need to make sure your policy doesn't exempt coverage beyond gliding distance of land. Although these may seem like extreme examples, ignoring these types of limitations or not knowing your policy details means that your insurance may not be required to cover any losses.

The most common reason people find themselves without coverage that applies is that they allow a non-approved pilot to operate the aircraft. Often, an "open-pilot warranty" is designated that sets forth minimum experience times that a non-owner pilot must have in order to be covered in the event of a claim. For example, a policy might require a pilot to have 25 hours of tailwheel time and 5 hours in make and model to be covered as a non-named pilot in a Cessna 170. If this is your aircraft, what if you let your buddy borrow it, and he has 300 hours of tailwheel time in a Cessna 195 but has never flown a Cessna 170? If your friend ground loops your Cessna 170 and damages a wing in the first hour of flying, you should expect that your coverage won't apply.

If you are going to let a friend use your aircraft, one way to ensure that your policy will cover that person is to ask that the insurer add a "named pilot" to your coverage. This will typically require the person to submit a "pilot history form" that details their individual experience. This will put an approval (if granted) on record for that specific individual, which will remove any question of coverage applicability.

Another common reason that coverage is not applicable is because an aircraft was being operated in a way not designated in the coverage purchased. An aircraft that was designated to be used for personal and business operations will find coverage hard to actuate if an accident happens while the aircraft was being rented out for flight training or used in a charter operation. Make sure the type of operation you will be conducting is designated in your coverage documents. If you are planning to change your use of the aircraft (e.g., become an agricultural sprayer), talk with your agent and update your coverage.

Although it may seem a bit capitalistic, the reality is that insurance companies are businesses. They make more money when they don't pay out claims. As an owner, if you want your insurance company to pay out when you need it, your job is to ensure that your operations are always within the contract guidelines that you agreed to for the coverage purchased.

To learn more about a few of the common reasons that insurance claims don't get paid, check out the Aircraft Owners and Pilots Association (AOPA) article, "5 Reasons Your Aviation Insurance Claim Could be Denied." (You can find the link to this article in the online Reader Resources at www.asa2fly.com/reader/avown).

Finding the Right Agent

Picking an insurance agent for your aircraft and flying activities can be as difficult, and as important, as choosing a business partner. All aircraft owners hope they will never end up having to use the insurance they purchase. But in the event that you do need to make a claim on your coverage, having the wrong coverage or an agent who doesn't know how to best fight for your needs and rights can be the difference that results in an unsatisfactory outcome—rather than the good outcome you want.

A key point to understand is that the "agent" will not typically be the person doing the "underwriting" of the insurance. An agent sells the policy and usually works with a number of underwriters who offer services. Direct agent/underwriters do exist, but many agents are separate businesses that offer agent services. The term "agent" means a person or business authorized to act on another's behalf—and the good news is that the insurance agent is *your* agent in the deal, not the agent of the underwriter. Their real job is to provide you, the client, with the services of securing and managing coverage for your aircraft.

You need to do a little homework before you pick an agent. Because you are limited to having only one "agent of record," it is important to make the right choice the first time. Switching agents can be nearly as difficult as breaking up a business partnership. Even if you simply want to shop for a new agent, you essentially must break up with the old one and sign a new agent of record agreement, which is required to allow a new agent to go out to the marketplace on your behalf.

Following are important considerations to think about when choosing an aviation insurance agent.

Does the agent specialize in aviation insurance?

You would be surprised how many owners have their business insurance agent try to go find them insurance for their aircraft. Most of these agents do not handle aviation insurance, so they must find another agent who then works with an underwriter to obtain the insurance. With this many middlemen, each taking a profit, the price increases. Find an agent who works directly with underwriters, which will help to keep the cost down and improve the service you receive. This will also increase the chance that the insurance you have in place will best serve your needs.

Does the agent understand your aircraft?

Some underwriters offer better pricing than others on particular aircraft makes and models. Make sure your agent understands your specific aircraft and knows what underwriter markets to shop in for your potential policy. This will help to ensure you get the best coverage for the best price.

Be willing to go outside the local area.

We are involved in aviation; remember that if we really need to meet in person, we can get in an airplane and fly somewhere to the meeting. Or if we just need to talk, there are always phones and digital conferencing options. Some of the best fits for insurance I have seen are instances in which people found insurance across the country from where they live or their businesses are operating.

You do not have to use the local agent in your town. Shop widely. If you were in need of a special surgery that no doctor in your town has ever done, you would go find a specialist somewhere else rather than let a local doctor give it a first try, right? You should do the same when you are shopping for an insurance representative for your aircraft and flying activities. If there is not a good, suitable agent where you operate, go find one somewhere else. Most brokerages are licensed in multiple states.

It isn't only about price.

Naturally, owners want to find the most cost-effective insurance policies they can to minimize costs, but choosing the *cheapest* policy may not result in the *best coverage*. It's necessary to find the right balance between the best value and the best coverage for how you will be utilizing your aircraft. The only way to do that is to find the right agent who will sell the best product for your needs.

Before you even have an agent "go out to the market" and get quotes from underwriters on your operation, take the time to shop around. Interview potential agents, ask for references, and talk with previous clients (with the agent's permission, of course) who have had claims managed by the agent or brokerage. If they aren't willing to allow you to ask these questions and will not provide some references, keep shopping. I promise that you can find a provider who will better meet your needs, even though you hope that you will never need to make an insurance claim.

Ways to Lower Your Insurance Premium

Everyone wants to know how to keep their premiums down and pay less every year. So, I would be remiss if I didn't share a few ways that you can accomplish that. Following are ideas that may help you lower your insurance premium.

Get More Experience

Generally speaking, insurance costs are lower for more experienced pilots. A private pilot who has just been certified will pay more for insurance on a V-tail Bonanza than will an ATP with 10,000 flight hours and 200 hours in make and model. This is because of the risk the underwriters have calculated each pilot represents based on their potential to have an accident. Therefore, the more experience you gain, the lower your premium will be. This does not mean that you will end up with free insurance when you hit the 100,000-hour mark. But more experience, more certifications, and more current training will help you be a lower risk and thus result in a lower premium.

Get Training

Beyond just getting certificates, ratings, and more flight hours, it will also help to get training specific to the make and model of aircraft you will be operating. In some aircraft, underwriters will require initial or recurrent training for a pilot on a scheduled frequency—often yearly, but sometimes every six months. For many aircraft, a pilot will be required to have a yearly instrument proficiency check (IPC) in the make and model to remain in compliance with the policy stipulations. Simulator-based training may also offer some reductions in premiums or, in some cases, may be required just to be covered at all.

Stay Actively Flying

Although it may sound counterintuitive, a more active pilot is actually a better bet for an underwriter than one who flies only a few times a year. Actively flying pilots will find themselves with lower premiums than those who fly only 10 hours per year. So it is to your benefit to go out and fly and to keep your agent up-to-date with yearly pilot history forms to ensure you receive the best rates when you renew the policy.

Remove Seats

While it will not change the hull value premium, removing seats in the aircraft will limit the potential passenger liability that an underwriter is exposed to by an accident. Many owners choose to remove seats in aircraft such as Cessna 210s in which the back seats are small and infrequently used, or in aircraft that have more seats than the weight and balance limits would realistically allow to be filled even with conservative fuel loads.

Keep in mind that if you remove seats from your aircraft, you also need to have an updated (and it can be a secondary) weight and balance that meets the new configuration to be operating in compliance with Federal Aviation Regulations (FARs).

In short, if you have an aircraft that has more seats than you will use, it may be worth removing some of them as this can result in premium savings.

Lower Insured Values

A balance here is important, but changing insured values will change the insurance premium. In general, lower hull values and lower liability limits will generate lower premium costs. But it is important to find the right balance between savings and risk, and this becomes a very personal choice based on the level of risk you are comfortable with or are able to take.

Chapter 4

Taxes and Your Aircraft

By Christopher Harper, CPA, MBA

Aircraft ownership can be expensive! Even though the adventure and personal satisfaction of operating a personal aircraft is worth the price of admission, prudent aviators seek opportunities to mitigate expenses. Many aircraft owners wonder if they can trim their individual or business income tax bills by deducting aviation-related expenses on their income tax returns. As with most tax questions, the answer depends upon each taxpayer's unique facts and circumstances. Aviators hoping to deduct expenses must know what information should be tracked, what questions to ask their advisors, and what circumstances they should contemplate before the acquisition of an aircraft. Prospective aircraft owners must include tax considerations alongside other financial realities as they assess resources available for the proper care and feeding of a private aircraft.

Owners may wonder about answers to questions like, "May I tax deduct the cost of my annual inspection? How about my hangar costs? Or the fuel I purchase when I fly from my home airport to a business meeting?" For many owners, their aircraft becomes a dual-use asset, which necessitates careful delineation regarding what may or may not be eligible to produce tax benefits.

An overarching tax question involves determining if the aircraft is a personal-use or business-use asset. Personal-use assets are not utilized in a trade or business operated in the pursuit of a profit. Rather, personal-use assets are owned for an individual's pleasure, recreation, or individual enjoyment. In contrast, business-use assets are placed into service by an individual or entity that is attempting to generate a profit (and thus taxable income). Federal income tax law generally prohibits deductions for personal-use assets but may allow deductions for business-use assets.

Sometimes this distinction is not binary. Although an aircraft might primarily be a personal-use asset (and therefore not deductible), the owner may occasionally use the asset in an income-generating activity. Just as you might occasionally use your personal automobile for business or employment-related activities, many aviators use their private aircraft for income-producing endeavors from time to time. Alternatively, an aircraft that is primarily a business-use asset may be used for personal purposes on occasion. The complexities of such mixed-use scenarios require special consideration because tax deductions may be limited, reimbursements might be excluded from taxable income, or the owner may need to include the value of personal flights in his or her personal tax calculations. Mixed-use scenarios complicate strategies that may already be nebulous in a world where tax decisions are rarely black and white!

Even if your aircraft is primarily a personal-use asset, you may find occasions when you use the asset for work or charitable purposes. Just as your employer may reimburse you for company use of your personal automobile using a cents-per-mile method, you may develop an arrangement that allows similar reimbursement when you use your aircraft for company purposes. There are also tax provisions that offer limited deductions for certain direct, out-of-pocket expenses when a taxpayer uses an aircraft for charitable purposes for a qualified 501(c)(3) organization.

Federal tax law typically allows taxpayers to deduct business-related expenses if they are "ordinary and necessary." Ordinary expenses are those that would typically be incurred by a prudent businessperson in a particular industry. Necessary expenses are appropriate and helpful in the taxpayer's pursuit of profit in a business activity. Most, if not all, of the expenses associated with an aircraft may be deductible if the asset is primarily used as an ordinary and necessary resource for a true business activity. Beware that certain expenditures may not be immediately deductible even if your aircraft is a business-use asset. For example, the acquisition cost of the aircraft and major improvements such as avionics will be subject to depreciation rules that may require the expenditures to be deducted over a number of years instead of being fully deductible in a single year.

Occasional personal utilization of a business-use aircraft requires additional scrutiny. Taxpayers may be required to include the value of personal flights in their individual taxable income if an aircraft is primarily owned for business purposes but is sometimes used for personal flights. Distinguishing business from personal use should be relatively straightforward because pilots routinely track flights in their logbooks.

Hobby loss rules could curtail your ability to deduct aviation-related expenditures and/or could invite scrutiny by the Internal Revenue Service (IRS). Expense deductions may be limited to the amount of revenue generated by a business activity if it looks more like a hobby than a profit-oriented business. The IRS will presume that an activity is truly a profit-seeking endeavor if it generates a profit in three out of five years. Failing this presumptive three-out-of-five-years test does not necessarily preclude the deduction of expenses that generate a tax loss. However, failing this presumptive test does place the burden of proof on the taxpayer to demonstrate that the activity has a true profit motivation. Examples of business-versus-hobby considerations include operating the activity in a businesslike manner, history of profit and losses, diversity of income streams, manner in which the activity is operated, time and effort expended on the activity, and success or failure operating similar ventures. Essentially, the IRS expects a profit-oriented activity to be operated in a manner that reflects the characteristics of a real business.

Although the IRS will typically consider business-versus-hobby characteristics in concert instead of focusing on a single element, one particular factor has noteworthy implications for aviation expenditures: the IRS will consider the amount of personal pleasure or recreational value derived from the activity. Aviators must beware that the potential for personal recreation has significant implications when considering whether aviation expenditures are incurred for a true profit-motivated activity or if they are primarily incurred for personal purposes.

Hobby loss rules could limit deductions when the aircraft is not primarily used in a profit- generating activity such as a charter or aircraft leasing operation. When hobby loss rules threaten the deductibility of expenditures, and to add complexity to the discussion, the Federal Aviation Regulations establish a hurdle that may be difficult for private pilots who hope to circumvent hobby loss limitations. Many factors that indicate profit motivation may run afoul of 14 CFR Part 135 rules that govern air carrier operations. For example, profit-oriented businesses actively seek revenue from a diverse customer base. Although earning revenue from many customers may cause an IRS auditor to look favorably upon your activity, the FAA could consider these factors indicative of a charter operation that would require an air carrier certificate. Aviators hoping to fully deduct aviation expenditures face a precarious journey as they straddle the IRS's hobby loss rules while steering clear of Part 135 requirements.

All these considerations come with an important side note: it is important to avoid problems with insurance coverage if you stray into a situation with a profit motivation. Private aircraft insurance policies typically provide coverage only for personal and business-related purposes where no charge is made for such flights. It is important for pilots to carefully examine their insurance policies to ensure that they do not invalidate insurance coverage by operating the aircraft for excluded purposes.

Leaseback arrangements present a possible strategy for defraying ownership costs while preserving income tax deductions. This may involve the owner purchasing the aircraft and then leasing the asset to an FBO, flight school, or other operator who offers the aircraft for rent to the general population of pilots (or student pilots) who meet certain eligibility criteria. Because leasing an asset is a profit-seeking activity, this arrangement typically allows deduction of ordinary and necessary ownership and operating expenses allowed by tax law. The owner usually will pay the established rental fee when he or she uses the aircraft. Although limited availability and sharing the aircraft with other renters are obvious drawbacks to this arrangement, owners realize that they will only be flying the aircraft for a fraction of the 8,760 hours available in a year. They may justify the arrangement because it can mitigate a portion of the fixed costs that would otherwise be sunk into idle time the aircraft would spend in a hangar. It is important for owners to understand that the IRS will consider aircraft rental to be passive activity income subject to limitations that will vary according to each taxpayer's individual circumstances. Owners should also consider the additional insurance premiums that will undoubtedly be required for an insurance policy that covers rental operations.

Regardless of the chosen tax strategies, aviators must resist the temptation to push limits or skirt tax laws and/or aviation regulations. Pilots should carefully document business versus non-business flights in their logbooks. Remember that IRS auditors can use FlightAware and other tracking tools, too!

A key consideration is that owners and operators of aircraft should track as much information as possible for their tax, legal, and other advisors. Document real fuel costs per flight, maintenance expenses, and upgrade costs. Keep a list of what flights were conducted and for what purpose, and keep a log of any storage or other costs. Get into the details and relay them to your advisors. Better recordkeeping doesn't necessarily mean all this information will generate a bigger tax deduction or refund, but this information certainly will not help your situation if you can't provide it at year-end because you have not maintained adequate records.

Saving tax dollars should not be a primary motivation for spending money on airplanes (or anything for that matter). Tax savings should be icing on the cake that helps defray the cost of ownership. Simply put, you probably cannot afford the aircraft if income tax deductions represent the tipping point in your ownership decision. Taxpayers should never spend money solely to generate a tax deduction; this is akin to giving someone one dollar just to have them give you 20, 30, or 40 cents in return. Aviators should have prudent non-tax motivations for expenditures that are made more palatable because of tax benefits.

This discussion likely created more questions than answers! This was intentional and represents the reality of today's complicated income tax and financial planning climate. This is a broad discussion of general topics; it would be impossible to address every scenario because each taxpayer's situation is influenced by myriad, nuanced variables. It is imperative that aircraft owners obtain advice from advisors who have examined their unique facts and circumstances.

Aviators must work closely with an accountant and aviation attorney to develop the most prudent strategies for their specific situation before acquisition and throughout their period of ownership. Because well-informed advisors give better advice than ill-informed advisors, aviators should be forthcoming with information. Explain how you intend to use the aircraft. Describe what, if any, business-related purposes you anticipate for flights. Explain the circumstances that may provide remuneration for flight costs (e.g., employer reimbursement or payments from a business entity that you own). Ask your accountant to recommend the best way to track expenses, reimbursements, revenues, and other financial activity. Work with your aviation attorney to determine if a corporation or limited liability company should own the aircraft. Don't forget to discuss the intended uses with your insurance broker to ensure that you purchase the appropriate type and level of coverage. Your outcome will be most satisfactory if you paint a realistic picture for your advisors so they may craft an ownership strategy that meets your needs while ensuring that you operate within guidelines that align with your personal situation. Thoughtful planning should give you peace of mind so you can enjoy your time in the air!

Christopher Harper works professionally as a Clinical Affiliate Instructor for the Seidman College of Business in the School of Accounting at Grand Valley State University (www.GVSU.edu) in Grand Rapids, Michigan, and is a Senior Manager at Hungerford Nichols CPAs + Advisors in Grand Rapids, Michigan (www. hungerfordnichols.com).

Harper is an active pilot who regularly uses his aircraft to fly for both business and pleasure. He has owned multiple general aviation aircraft over the years, and at the time of this writing is the owner of a Piper Twin Comanche and partners with a friend on a Piper Cherokee 6.

Chapter 5

Picking the Right Airport to Call Home

Choosing an airport is not just about finding a hangar at the airport closest to your home. At least it shouldn't be. Finding the right airport to call home can greatly affect the quality of your aviation experience, impact how often you will be able to use your airplane, and even determine who you will meet that might become your friends.

An airport is not just a location with a hangar to store your plane. An airport is also a community, a place where you will (hopefully) be able to secure services for your aircraft, and a place you may end up calling home for a long time.

Often when pilots buy airplanes, the task of finding a hangar or the services they need at a particular airport becomes an afterthought—something they will consider and investigate once they have already purchased the aircraft. Having a place to put your airplane when you take delivery is something to consider before the purchase is made. This may make the difference not only in whether your aircraft is protected but also in whether you will be able to use the aircraft at your leisure or need.

Depending on where you are located, there may be only a limited number of airports that are within a reasonable distance of where you live and that are suitable for basing your aircraft, but if there is more than one, it is worth taking some time to compare them.

Naturally, you would hope that finding the right home for your aircraft won't mean basing it at a distant airport that requires you to spend more time driving there than you will flying your airplane. However, the best place for your airplane will not always be the closest airport, either. You may discover that being willing to drive a little farther is a better option if it means you'll find the right airport facilities, services, and community.

A variety of factors should be considered when looking for a home for your airplane. These include airport considerations such as FBO and fueling services, maintenance services, aircraft storage, infrastructure, airspace and approaches, security, emergency services, other airport users, and the feel of the airport community. These are covered in the following sections.

FBO and Fueling Services

The services available at the airport, whether they are provided by a fixed base operator (FBO) or the local municipality, make a big difference. Even something as basic as fuel might be available intermittently, only during normal business hours, or maybe not at all. The other services available at the airport establish the level of support services you will be able to expect for your flight operations. Some may be more important than others depending on your regular use.

Fuel Services

Not every airport has the same systems for fuel delivery for tenants. Fuel may be provided by trucks from FBOs, it may be available from credit card-actuated self-service pumps, or I have even seen fuel available 24 hours a day from pumps that work on the honor system where pilots log their pumped fuel and are billed later by the airport. Fortunately, most pilots are pretty darn honest.

When analyzing services available at an airport, it's important to consider the availability of fuel. Does the FBO provide fuel that is full-service or is self-service fuel available? You might be comfortable fueling your own aircraft, but will you always want to?

Many pilots prefer to have the staff of an FBO provide full-service fueling for their aircraft. This can certainly save you time. It's also a nice service to have when it is cold outside. If you call ahead, an FBO can often complete the fueling before you even get out to your aircraft, giving you the opportunity to save some time and effort by having your plane fueled before you arrive.

At airports where both self-service and full-service fueling options exist, full-service fueling may cost a little more per gallon than self-service fuel pumps. At some airports, only full-service fueling is available. In these cases, it may be critical to learn if fueling is available 24 hours a day. It can be extremely frustrating to show up to the airport for an early departure at 5:00 a.m. when you need fuel only to find out that the local FBO doesn't have any staff in the office until 8:00 a.m. If this type of fuel availability will be a regular need for the operation of your aircraft, an airport with those limitations perhaps isn't the best one to call home.

When airports have self-service fueling systems, this can remove timing issues as a consideration and it may be easier to fulfill your fueling needs, assuming the fueling systems work 24 hours a day. Many airports have self-actuated fuel pumps that can be operated via credit card. In these cases, fueling is generally available at most times. However, one danger of these systems is that if they fail for any reason while airport staff is not around, you may not be able to get fuel. Many of these systems are notorious for failing in very cold conditions and when blowing snow gets into their card readers.

I still see many airports at which fuel is only available when the FBO is open, for pilots who have accounts with the airport, or for pilots who have keys to the locks on the fuel pumps. Although it might sound surprising, at many smaller airports, it's not cost-effective to install expensive credit card-operated fuel pump systems.

It is also worth finding out who provides the fuel at the airport. While FBOs provide fuel at many airports, especially larger ones, at some airports the fuel is provided by the municipality that owns the airport. Cities, townships, and counties that operate airports frequently offer fuel at their airports at much lower profit margins than FBOs. This is regularly done as a way to promote use of an airport and entice aircraft owners to base their planes at these fields.

Completing a quick survey of local airport fueling prices over a few months of history can help you determine if some local airports typically have higher fuel prices than others. While a price difference may seem minimal on any single tank of gas, when it's added up over multiple years of aircraft operations, even twenty-five cents per gallon can make a difference in the bottom line for your aircraft costs.

Although it is uncommon, pilots may in some cases be allowed to bring in their own fuel. Most airports do not allow the storage of fuel in hangars due to the fire danger it represents, but personal tanks are allowed in rare cases. If this is something you want to consider, be sure to inquire with airport management about airport, local municipal, and state or federal rules and regulations that might be applicable.

FBO/Common Area Services

One of my rules of flying has always been to visit the bathroom before a flight to reduce the chance of needing one en route. Does the airport where you are considering basing your aircraft have available bathrooms? It might seem like a pretty simple thing, but if the bathroom is inside an FBO or an airport building that is closed during off-hours, you may find yourself needing alternatives.

Some airports have porta-potties out near hangars if they are away from the main service areas of the airport. These portable bathrooms can become very warm (and smelly) in the summer in hot climates and very cold in the winter.

At certain airports, common areas or buildings are available to resident tenant hangars, but these areas may require codes or keys for access. If you are a considering such an airport, be sure to look into what it takes to get access to these areas.

In many states, public buildings are available at airports for all users. Some states leave these buildings open at all times and others provide common access codes that pilots will need to gain access. For example, codes are commonly set to airport runway numbers or local frequencies, giving pilots an easy way to remember the codes for access to the public buildings.

Common areas in FBOs that are accessible to local or transient pilots can be used for meeting passengers, planning flights, calling for weather briefings, or just relaxing a bit before or after a flight.

Many local airports have common areas that become gathering points for local pilots and sometimes offer cooking facilities—or at least a coffee pot and vending machine for pop or snacks. Common areas in standalone buildings or within FBOs will often provide rest areas for pilots to use between flights, computers for obtaining weather information, and tables to sit at for meals, among other offerings. If you are considering basing your airplane at an airport that does not have any of these amenities, you may find yourself trying to complete these tasks in your car or on the wing of an airplane in a cold hangar.

Larger airports will typically have larger FBOs that offer more services. But in some cases, smaller local airports have great FBOs that offer a similar level of services, although this is less common. On the other hand, larger FBOs at big airports might be focused on corporate customers while an FBO at a smaller, local airport might be more focused on providing service to smaller aircraft with individual owners. Consider what type and level of service you will want from an FBO, as this may also affect the size of the airport you consider for your aircraft's home.

Training Areas

Are you going to be receiving any instruction? If so and if you are using your own aircraft, it may be very awkward to receive training in the middle of an FBO that also rents aircraft and provides training. It would be even more awkward and potentially even rude to receive training from an instructor that is not employed by the local FBO.

Consider what facilities might be available for you to use if you will need additional training. For example, this might include considering open common areas you could use to meet with an instructor or learning what services the local FBO can provide for instruction.

Examining all the factors that make a good training environment would take a much more detailed discussion, but when you are looking at which airport to call home, think about your needs and what will work for you.

Aircraft Servicing

In addition to aircraft maintenance services (covered later in this chapter), it can be helpful to have other services available from the FBO. Many local FBOs will wash and wax your airplane for a fee if you want. Of course, this is something that you can do yourself, but do you really like crawling under your aircraft and getting soaked while you scrub the belly? Wouldn't it be better to let the local high school kid working for the FBO earn a few bucks washing your plane while you sip lemonade on a hot summer day? You might also decide that it's worth paying someone to clean your windshield for you.

Aircraft readiness services can also save time. Many FBOs will pull out and put away your aircraft for a fee, as part of a yearly service package, or sometimes as a service included in your hangar fees. This can save you both time and lots of tugging to drag your aircraft in or out of a hangar. If you are in a community hangar or a one that an FBO uses to store multiple aircraft, you may not even be allowed to pull out or put away your own aircraft.

Rental Aircraft Availability

Once they own an airplane, many pilots think they will never need to rent an aircraft again, but this is not always the case. When your airplane is down for maintenance (even for annuals or 100-hour inspections), you may want to have access to rental aircraft during the downtime.

You may also encounter times when an aircraft that is different than the one you own is a better fit for your particular flight needs, so you might even want to look into what rental aircraft are available at the airports you are considering. For example, if you own a two- or four-seat, single-engine aircraft, choosing to locate at an airport that has larger (e.g., six-seat) or twin-engine aircraft may offer you the option to use one of these different aircraft to meet your needs for special, occasional flights that are outside of normal operations for your aircraft.

Available Maintenance Services

The airport you call home is the place where your airplane usually will be when most maintenance needs pop up. You might be able to fly elsewhere to have your annual inspection completed, but when something breaks, your aircraft may not always be flyable. Having competent maintenance services available on site can make it much easier to get your aircraft airworthy again.

When looking at airports in your local area, it is important to consider what maintenance services are available at each and whether they have any restrictions on maintenance provisions. Not all airports have maintenance providers, so if you are based at one without maintenance services and something is wrong with your airplane, you may have a hard time getting service for it.

In addition, restrictions may be present in hangar rental agreements prohibiting maintenance from being conducted in rental hangars. It is better to find this out before rather than after you have committed to a specific airport and hangar, as the latter might result in a much more expensive process to get necessary maintenance completed on your aircraft.

In picking the right airport, however, it doesn't mean that the maintenance provider on the field is the one that you must use as the primary service provider for your aircraft. The chapter on maintaining your aircraft includes more details on this point. With this in mind, it is worth noting that having a maintenance provider at the airport can make it much easier to fix an aircraft when it is unable to be flown to another provider.

Rented Aircraft Storage (and Hangars)

Part of owning an airplane is that you will need a place to store it (along with the many other things that typically go with your plane), and there are lots of options. Most pilots rent hangars from the airport (often the municipality that owns the airport) or developers that build hangars at the airport for rental income. The most common types include box hangars, nested T-hangars, and what are basically upsized car ports that are open except for the roof. Each of these offers cover for airplanes, but each type will not necessarily meet the needs of every pilot.

When looking at airports, finding the right place to store your aircraft is important for the protection of your plane and for keeping it ready to fly when you need it. Visit multiple airports and find out what types of storage options are available at each of them. In some locations, hangar space is at a premium, and pilots may need to be placed on a waiting list for hangar space as it becomes available. In these cases, pilots might decide to base their aircraft at airports farther away where space is available instead of leaving their aircraft out on the ramp until storage space opens up.

Price is also a consideration for many. Hangar space is commonly more expensive in urban environments and at larger, busier airports. Being willing to drive even 30 minutes to an airport farther from these areas may allow pilots to find significant savings in their storage costs.

It's also worth taking the time to look through ground lease or hangar rental agreements to make sure that your intended use is not in any way in breach of the covenants of these agreements.

Chapter 6 provides you with much more detail about evaluating aircraft storage options and selecting the best one to meet your particular needs.

Airport Infrastructure

The actual infrastructure of the airport should also make a difference in your decision of what airport to call home. Important factors to consider include runway lengths, whether it has multiple runways, whether it is towered or non-towered, what kind of snow removal is available, and other inclement weather factors that might affect your operations.

Towered versus Non-Towered

A first infrastructure consideration might be whether the airport has an operational control tower. Typically, towered airports are found in Class D, Class C, or Class B airspace. These airports have higher traffic densities than many smaller, local airports. This traffic can be harder to work within for some pilots, but at the same time, a towered airport may offer services not available at non-towered airports.

Towered airports (during tower operation hours) can help provide pilots with services for instrument flight, including but not limited to opening and closing flight plans, receiving and granting IFR clearances, and even something as simple as allowing special VFR clearances for a little traffic pattern work when the visibility is down.

The ATC staff in the tower also help to provide awareness of and separation from other traffic as pilots operate within their airspace. This extra set of eyes can help keep you safer as you fly at a towered airport. Operations at towered airports do require more communication (with ATC) for movement of your aircraft around the field. This is not only for operations such as takeoff and landing but also for runs to fuel pumps, taxiing over to the FBO, or other smaller tasks. While many pilots are fearful of the extra "radio work" that is required at a towered airport, most pilots acclimate quickly.

It might be uncommon to find a home for your aircraft at a large Class B airport (e.g., places like Atlanta-Hartsfield, Chicago O'Hare, Dallas-Ft. Worth, or Washington Dulles), but it is not uncommon for pilots to find good homes at Class C or Class D airports. Many Class C and Class D airspace-covered airports are not terribly busy but offer great services to pilots.

In the case of a Class C airport or one in a terminal radar service area (TRSA), added radar service may even offer a greater possible level of integration service into the national airspace system for a pilot that travels and files IFR regularly. Many of these larger airports will also have bigger FBOs that offer more services to tenants on the field.

If your primary focus on flying is to fly VFR for a little pattern work or just take Sunday morning trips around your local area, the extra services available from a towered airport may not be necessary or even desired.

Non-towered airports are typically a little less restrictive regarding movements of aircraft but also have less to offer from ATC. While radio communication is recommended, it is not necessarily required. Few non-towered airports are served by air carrier services that may require additional security procedures.

Many non-towered airports have a stronger feeling of community that develops between the pilots and tenants than at more formalized, larger airports. Access at non-towered airports is often easier for both pilots and their guests. Restrictions on driving to hangars may be less restrictive at smaller airports, especially those in rural areas or at non-air carrier serviced airports.

Runways

Runways are an obvious factor to consider in evaluating airports. The most basic question is whether or not the runway(s) at the airport are long enough for the aircraft that you will operate. If the runway lengths are too short, it should be obvious that the airport is not the right one to call home. Another potential consideration is the number of available runways.

A friend of mine bases his airplane at an airport that has one runway in a generally north-south alignment. Unfortunately, the predominant winds at this airport are out of the west—meaning a direct crosswind on most days. While the airport had to align the runway this way due to property restrictions, nearby towers, and to maximize the runway length, it does make it harder for pilots who are less accustomed to flying with strong crosswinds. If you own a tailwheel aircraft, you might choose to find an airport that encounters fewer crosswind days.

Barring other factors that force particular runway alignments, it is common for most airports to align their runways with prevailing winds. In fact, the FAA prefers that airport runways be aligned within 30 degrees of the prevailing winds in an effort to help reduce potential crosswind dangers.

Crosswinds can also be mitigated by basing your aircraft at an airport with multiple runways. In addition, multiple runways can offer an opportunity for multiple instrument approaches to the airport, which can allow a pilot to more successfully find the airport in IFR conditions.

It's not impossible to find out what prevailing winds are at an airport you are considering. In fact, the National Oceanic and Atmospheric Association (NOAA) tracks and publishes wind data at many sites around the country.

To research the prevailing winds at your airport, visit www.climate.gov/teaching/resources/wind-map.

You should also check out the overall condition of the runways. Does it look like the airport is being well maintained? Poor-quality runways can increase potential maintenance concerns and costs for your aircraft as well as affect safety.

What about sod runways? Not all airport runways are paved, and this is a good thing for some pilots and aircraft. A Piper Cub or an Aeronca Champ just feels better on sod to me. If you will be flying a classic aircraft that almost begs to be on a nicely cut sod runway, perhaps seeking out a place that offers one will be better than choosing a more urban, pavement-clad airport.

Environmental Effects

The environment can have a significant effect on the usability of the airport. In northern climates, snow removal can be a factor in how many days a year an airport is usable. The airport infrastructure and how it is maintained can affect how well the airport will serve your needs.

Many smaller airports have snow removal conducted by local municipal vehicles that are also responsible for plowing roads. This can mean that clearing snow from the airport becomes a secondary priority, which can result in the airport not being cleared immediately after a storm or early in the morning. If you will be using your aircraft for early morning or all-weather operations, this kind of airport is probably not the best choice to call home. Airports with dedicated snow removal equipment are more likely to have runways, taxiways, and hangar areas cleared in a timelier manner.

It is also worth assessing how well the snow removal is conducted. Aircraft with longer wings, twin-engine aircraft, or aircraft that require larger turning radii may encounter problems if snow banks are not pushed back, or if corners at taxiways or entrances to hangar areas (and hangar areas themselves) are not sufficiently cut down or blown clear to allow ground navigation to or from airport operations areas.

Snow is not the only potential environmental problem that you might encounter at airports. In some places, flooding can also be a concern. At an airport I visited in California that was below the floodplain for the area, it flooded almost every year. Tenants at the airport regularly had to move their aircraft during periods of flooding, sometimes with very short notice. If you find any pictures showing a particular airport underwater on a regular basis, perhaps another location would be better for your home base.

Other considerations might include dust and wind. In areas where flood or snow conditions aren't really a problem, it is possible that windy, dusty environments can be detrimental to aircraft. If you are looking at an airport in one of these areas and plan to leave your airplane under awning coverage or even tied down on the ramp, consider how a windy, dusty field might affect the paint on your aircraft over time. In these locations, hangar storage might be required in order to reduce wear and tear on your aircraft.

Airspace and Approaches for All-Weather Access

For pilots who will be flying beyond basic VFR conditions, the types of instrument approaches available at an airport can be important. If your aircraft does not have an IFR-capable GPS and the only approaches available at an airport are GPS-based, these approaches will not do you any good.

Evaluate the capabilities of your aircraft and make sure the airport at which you will be based has applicable approaches. If they don't have approaches you can use, you may need to be willing to divert to other nearby airports and then get a ride when the weather deteriorates.

Currently, GPS approaches are most commonly available at many airports. VOR approaches are still available in many locations, and some airports maintain ILS approaches. Typically, but not always, ILS or other localizer-type approaches will be found at larger airports. It is also becoming more common for precision (LPV, LP, or LNAV/VNAV) GPS approaches to be found at general aviation served airports. These approaches allow pilots to fly to lower minimums safely, increasing the number of days a capable aircraft will be able to get to its destination with a current and competent pilot.

Thus, when you are considering airports, make sure to take a thorough look through the approaches at each airport as well as other nearby airports, as this can be a determining factor to consider as a savvy pilot.

Airspace may also be a consideration in choosing where to base your aircraft. If you are planning on purchasing an aerobatic aircraft to practice in, such as a Pitts or an Extra, the closer you are to airspace that can be used for aerobatic maneuvers, the less transition flight will be needed before you can have some fun.

If you have a classic aircraft that does not have a transponder, it probably doesn't make sense to home it at an airport that lies within a Mode C ring or in Class C or B airspace. The same would hold true if your aircraft does not have a radio that allows communication with ATC. Some airports are within military operations areas (MOAs) or even Restricted areas that may hinder a pilot's operational options. For example, if you happen to live in the Washington, D.C., area, some important restrictions are present around the metro area (i.e., a Special Flight Rules Area) and nearby is a prohibited area (Camp David) that regularly expands to a temporary flight restriction (TFR) some 30 miles in size. If your airport happens to be in this area, you may find yourself grounded when you are looking to fly.

Check out the airspace that is directly present at the airport, overlies the airport, or even is near the airport to determine if any of the restrictions will hamper your flying needs and desires.

Airport Security

Security at airports has become a greater concern over time, and this trend will likely continue for the foreseeable future. When considering which airport to call home, the types of security procedures in place can be a factor that sways a pilot toward one airport or another.

Airports serving air carriers typically have more security procedures in place than airports that do not serve air carriers. It is common for airports that have air carrier service to require individual-specific badging. Guests will commonly have to be escorted by a badged individual and vehicles may have to be registered and authorized to drive into secured areas of the airport. Some pilots consider this a hassle and prefer to base their aircraft at airports that have less stringent security procedures.

Airports in urban environments will commonly have full perimeter security fences, while many rural airports may not even have gates barring people from driving onto active areas of the airfield. These certainly represent two extremes, and fortunately, most people are good-enough citizens to not drive down runways at airports where no security perimeter exists.

Airports with a less significant security presence will cause fewer delays in access to your aircraft, will make it easier for your passengers and guests, and are less restrictive of your activities as a pilot while on the airfield. At many more rural airports, your dog may be welcome to run around the infield as you play fetch, but the actual security for your aircraft may be reduced. If your aircraft is in a hangar, the only security for your aircraft and belongings may be the lock on the hangar door.

Airports with greater levels of security may have more protection to offer for your aircraft by reducing the ability of unauthorized individuals to gain access to areas of the airfield where hangars are located. While the security is enhanced, the tradeoff may be a reduction in some of the personal liberties that can be enjoyed at less-structured airports.

In regard to security, there is a balance that you have to consider, and then you need to become comfortable with whatever option you choose. How fearful are you that someone may gain access to your hangar? How much of a hassle do you consider more stringent security procedures? The choice really is up to you.

Other Users of the Airport

Unless you have built your own airport, you probably won't be the only one using it. Other airport users can affect the level of attention you receive for your own needs, what areas of the airport you can access, and what level of security will be present.

At airports that have larger corporate operators, the attention given to these operators' fueling needs might always come before those of smaller general aviation (GA) aircraft pilots. This is just a reality of business. At airports with air carrier service, departure clearances for airlines on schedules may rise to a greater level of importance than getting the pilot out flying his Mooney.

If you are based at an airport that shares the runway with a National Guard base, then takeoffs, landings, and pattern work clearance for a KC-135 Stratotanker may leave heavy wake turbulence that would be rough on a Cessna 150 owner looking to get in a little pattern work at the same time.

At an airport where a large flight school is based, a Bonanza pilot could discover that the pattern is full of students who are having difficulty learning to make radio calls (don't judge them; we all had to learn somehow).

What about an airport that is also the base of an active skydiving drop zone? This might require other pilots to coordinate more carefully with obstacles falling through the airport surface as they try to practice instrument approaches. Gliders based at the airport will require a Seneca pilot to adjust his pattern to allow the slower and less maneuverable aircraft to have priority in a traffic pattern during landing.

While any one pilot might be fine with some or all of these situations, others may not be comfortable with them. Take the time to check the *Chart Supplements U.S.* and visit the airport to learn more about what types of operations are present on the field. Doing so will keep you from being surprised by something that may later become a frustration or even reduce the utility you can get from your use of the airport.

Emergency Services

While you hope you will never need them, having emergency services available at the airport might end up being the difference between life and death.

Larger airports will commonly have more robust emergency services facilities than smaller airports. In most rural airports, no services are available, and the emergency response after a crash or fire would be dependent on the local volunteer fire department.

Although as pilots, we certainly don't plan to need these for every flight, if there comes a time when we do need them, it can be invaluable to know what services are available. If the services aren't based on the field, just knowing who will provide them—and who to call in the event of a runaway engine fire or sliding off the runway in icy conditions—can be the difference between a long or a short response time.

Private Airports

While they are not right for everyone, private airports can sometimes be good options. A few private airports function as fly-in communities where pilots live and fly right from their backyards. Many private airports offer the availability of aircraft storage, ramp space, and other options for pilots. In many of these airports, the sense of community is very strong since they typically are very focused toward general aviation. While most private airports will not have large FBOs and many do not have instrument approaches available, the sense of community can be a major draw for pilots. Near urban areas, private airports in the suburbs can offer a little island of general aviation in the middle of larger, more corporate or airline-centric aviation interests. Taking some time to contact local private airports, if they exist, may produce surprisingly good options for many GA pilots.

Community

One aspect of being a pilot is that once you are certified, you will be part of an overall aviation community forever. Inside that big community, each individual airport may have a slightly different feel as a local community. Finding the airport that has the right feel for you can mean the difference between being a pilot who comes in and out without getting to know anyone and being part of a community with hangar barbecues where you can make lasting friends for a lifetime in aviation.

There are ways you can learn about the community at an airport to help you decide if it will be the right "fit" for you and your aircraft. Find out if the pilots at the airport have regular meetings. These might be meetings of clubs such as a local Experimental Aircraft Association (EAA) chapter, meetings of airport advisory boards, or just informal meetings of pilots on Saturday mornings for coffee, donuts, and a bit of hangar talk. Becoming a member of these activities can help you get to know other pilots who might be good safety pilots, meet pilots you can join for fly-outs to other airport events, and get involved with airport projects and events.

Learn more about how the airport is run. A dictatorial airport manager might make it difficult to have as much fun. Talk with local pilots about what it is like to be a pilot at the airport. Ask them what things they would like to change, which will help you discover any potential speed bumps that might make you want to reconsider choosing the airport.

Dropping by on a nice Saturday morning or afternoon will let you see if there are open hangar doors with other pilots hanging around who you could get to know. There is something special about sharing some time over a barbecue with a next-door hangar tenant while chatting about aviation. If you are someone who wants to build an airplane, finding an airport with other homebuilders on site can end up becoming a resource. Groups of builders motivate each other to keep making progress. Even just having other pilots to help celebrate your building progress can have a positive effect.

The community feel of an airport can make the difference between whether the airport becomes a home away from home with close friends or just a cold place that happens to house your aircraft. Consider what you really need and what is going to help feed the aviation needs of your soul.

. . .

When it comes down to selecting an airport to call home, it's about finding the best fit for you and your aircraft. While there are many factors to consider, you probably won't be able to get everything you want at any single airport. However, you can try to prioritize what is most important for you and how you will use your airplane. By doing this, you can evaluate local airports and find the one that will make the best home for your plane and for your flying.

Chapter 6

What to Look for in Aircraft Storage (Hangars and More)

Choosing the right storage option for your aircraft is a big part of picking the right airport, and there are many storage options to consider. The first question to ask—which is probably obvious—is do you need a hangar at all or would some type of tie-down or other coverage option be sufficient? Secondly, will your chosen aircraft fit in the space? Beyond these basic questions, the options begin to diverge and require some evaluation on the part of the aircraft owner.

Outdoor Options

In some locations, it may not be necessary to keep your aircraft inside at all times. In places where heavy rains or snow are uncommon, it may be just fine to keep your aircraft out on a ramp in a tie-down. Typically, tie-down storage is the most affordable option that will be available, but it offers the least protection for an aircraft. Tie-downs at many rural airports are even free.

Tie-down storage may be a good temporary option for pilots to use while they wait for hangar space to become available at the same or another airport. This storage may also be desirable if the aircraft won't be based at a particular airport for a long period of time for other reasons.

An aircraft left outside in tie-downs for lengthy periods of time will experience greater weathering effects on paint, will subject aircraft instruments to large fluctuations in temperature, and may affect other aircraft systems such as landing gear or control surfaces and mechanisms. High winds, heavy rain, and blowing sand or snow can greatly increase the wear and tear on an aircraft over time. If your aircraft is already in need of a paint job, this may be of less concern than if you just had a fresh paint job done and want to protect your investment for a long time to come.

When contemplating tie-downs as an option for your aircraft storage, also consider that your aircraft potentially may not be as secure as it would be in a locked hangar. Many airports (especially rural ones) have nothing that limits access to the airport ramp areas. If you are going to leave your aircraft on an airport ramp that does not limit access only to pilots and their passengers, it is a good idea to install aircraft door and baggage-area locks and use a prop lock device.

While these steps won't eliminate any and all risks to your aircraft, they will minimize the potential that your aircraft will be a quick and easy target for theft or damage. Many owners who have left their aircraft unlocked on unsecured ramps have returned to find missing avionics or other components that were removed overnight. There's no doubt that these can easily find their way onto eBay or other similar places where goods are sold with little check on who is selling them.

An open ramp or a hangar may not necessarily be the only two options available. In some areas, carport-style awnings can be good alternatives to further protect aircraft from the elements. These are storage structures that do not have walls but have roofs that will cover an aircraft. While these may not eliminate all blowing snow or wind effects on your aircraft, they do provide a solid cover to eliminate hail damage or heavy snow accumulation.

Carport-style aircraft storage facilities are typically set up in a pattern of nested T-shaped spaces where aircraft are pushed back into an assigned spot, which may or may not additionally include tie-downs under the roof. Unlike parking on an open ramp, these provide basic roof protection for the aircraft and also commonly have overhead lighting (although it's not always the brightest). This can certainly make preflighting before a flight or securing an aircraft after a long day of flying easier than completing these tasks in the dark with a flashlight.

Carport-style storage does not necessarily limit access to an aircraft's contents like a hangar does, but it can provide an option to lock your aircraft to a fixed structure (the posts or the trusses of the building) via chain to hinder any would-be aircraft thieves. Just don't forget to remove any installed locking mechanisms prior to taxiing away for your next flight!

If one of these outdoor storage options is not what you are looking for because they don't offer enough protection or security, it probably means that a hangar is what you want. There are many different styles and configurations of hangars that might be available at your location. A little understanding and research will allow you to find the best one for you and your aircraft.

General Hangar Considerations

Hangars are designed to provide aircraft with full protection from the elements and provide aircraft security intended to reduce the risk of theft or damage. Beyond this, many of the options and features offered by various hangar styles are a matter of taste, desire for additional comforts and features, and budget.

Electricity

Electricity is a basic feature, but not all hangars offer it. The availability of electricity allows pilots to have additional lighting, to plug in ancillary tools they might want to use, to charge batteries, or to plug in an aircraft if an oil pan or engine heater is needed for preheating prior to flight. But electricity is not a mandatory item for many aircraft owners who just want four walls of protection and a lockable door for security of their aircraft.

In some cases, electricity is provided at no additional charge to the hangar tenant, but in other cases each hangar will have its own meter and tenants will be responsible for their own billing separate from their hangar rent. Naturally, if a hangar is owned by an individual, that person would be expected to pay for that hangar's electricity usage.

Although it might go without saying, I think it's important to note that if there is not electricity, don't expect the hangar door(s) to be powered. In that case, there will be some sort of manually operated door that will need to be pushed, pulled, or cranked to open and close it.

Hangar Doors

Doors on hangars vary widely from sliding or rolling manual doors to fully electric bi-fold or horizontally opening doors. Naturally, the bigger the hangar is, the bigger the door usually is. When considering doors on hangars, one of the basic considerations is obviously to evaluate if the width and height available when the hangar door is open is sufficient to allow the aircraft to be pushed inside.

Although it might seem like electric doors would always be better, this isn't necessarily the case. What happens when the electricity fails? Manual doors are less likely to fail and leave a pilot with their aircraft stuck in a hangar until a fix can be made. On too many occasions, I have found myself with a broken hangar cable or a burned-out hangar door motor on a Friday night with a full schedule of flying over the weekend, and I've been unable to get needed parts until Monday morning.

Electrically powered doors that have a cable system that wraps around an axle to retract the doors (typically bi-fold) require attention to the cables. As these cables wear through usage, they break. Although a door can sometimes be operated with a broken cable, in most cases a cable break means that the door will remain in position until a fix can be made. Many cable doors have multiple cables that need to be monitored and maintained.

Other bi-fold doors may have a chain system that is electrically actuated to lift the door. While these systems are less likely to experience a breakage, the chains can sometimes come off track if not maintained properly. These chains, typically on either side of the door, require some greasing and maintenance to keep them operating smoothly. And I can attest from personal experience that it can be a really unhappy place to get a finger stuck when someone actuates a door unexpectedly.

Chains and cables are too small to handle the weight of lifting bigger doors, and so these doors will typically slide to the side or into a pocket in the front part of the hangar. It is common for larger doors to be moved by electrically powered wheels (with motors) that sit on tracks to guide the doors. The most common failure points of these systems include blockages of tracks (sometimes even from snow, ice, dirt, or rocks), which can cause the doors to slip or derail, affecting proper operation.

Weather Considerations

With any type of hangar doors, the most common frustration encountered by pilots is blockage by snow and ice in areas that experience cold winters. The harsher the winters, the worse this problem can be. Iced-up hangar doors, piled-up snow in front of doors, or worse, snowbanks from snow-removal operations can leave a pilot forced to manually remove the obstructions.

It is a good idea to have a sturdy snow shovel and something to chip ice if your hangar is in an area with strong winters. Also be sure to plan ahead and leave enough time prior to a planned departure to remove these obstructions, or even go out the day before and get it done. Two hours of chipping ice and shoveling snow before a flight can leave a pilot tired, cold, and wet. This is not a fun situation to be in when leaving on an important trip—especially when you end up having to clear ice and snow in dress clothes and shoes.

Heating and Cooling

Heat in hangars is another potential creature comfort. So is air conditioning. In colder climates, heat can be important for keeping an aircraft engine warm and for keeping the pilot comfortable when working in the hangar. It can also keep doors from freezing in place and minimize the amount of snow that accumulates directly in front of the doors. The type of heat available at any given hangar will vary based on the type of utilities available at the airport. It is worth considering the costs of heating a hangar and balancing that against the benefits it will provide.

Common heating options include radiant heaters in the ceiling, forced air heaters, or heated floors in some cases. Heaters can be powered by natural gas, propane, or electricity. I have even seen a few northern hangars heated by wood-burning stoves. While this can be very cheap, it does come with the added work of cutting the wood to feed the furnace! When considering a heated hangar, a savvy hangar shopper should ask for samples of the heating bills from the previous year to better gauge how much they will need to budget for hangar heating costs.

The larger the hangar door, the more heat that will escape in the winter when the door is opened. This can be extremely expensive. One friend of mine who has a large hangar in northern Canada and operates a cargo-hauling operation also periodically provides hangar space to transient aircraft. If the transient aircraft operators want to open the door at a time other than when the cargo operation needs it open for its own operations, they will be charged $600 every time the door is opened during the winter. This may seem excessive, but my friend has done the math and determined that is the cost each time they open a hangar door in the well-below-zero temperatures in northern Canada.

If your aircraft is in a single-aircraft hangar, you will probably have more control over the heating options but will also be responsible for the entire heating bill. Most of the time, unless your hangar is also a workshop or a pilot hideout with lounging areas, just keeping the hangar over the freezing point is probably adequate. By keeping a hangar in the low 40-degree range, this will generally be sufficient to keep an engine warm, keep avionics warm, and make preflighting operations comfortable.

Many of the same considerations come into play in the opposite environmental extreme with air conditioning in hangars. In extremely warm climates, either very large fans or air conditioning may be available options. While there is no need to preheat engines in these climates, it is much more comfortable to preflight in a 70-degree hangar than in one that has been baking in 110-degree heat under the desert southwest sun. Again, frequently opening and closing doors will be a way to lose efficiency and spend much more on utility costs.

Insulation can be one way to reduce utility costs for both heating and air conditioning systems. If the hangar is already insulated, that's fantastic. If it isn't, upgrading and installing insulation can be a fast and relatively cost-effective means of reducing utility costs with a quick return on investment. Even if a hangar is a rental, the owner may be more than willing to allow you to invest in adding insulation. If you plan to rent the hangar for a long period of time (i.e., years), this may be worth your effort and investment.

Flooring, Drainage, and Slope

The type of hangar flooring can also be a matter of concern in rare cases. At some airports, gravel or even dirt floors still exist in some hangars. This can make it difficult to pull an aircraft in and out. Additionally, the floors can become muddy if any flooding comes in under the doors. Although most floors will be cement or potentially asphalt, it is worth checking to confirm what type of flooring is used before you commit.

Drainage may also be worth evaluating. I have seen hangars that have seemingly good cement floors but that end up flooding every time it rains because door seals are bad or drainage from a ramp travels up against the building. This can affect what you might be able to store in the hangar or whether you can count on having a dry, clean floor to work on in the location where you store your aircraft.

Although it is easy to overlook, it's a good idea to check if the entrance to the hangar happens to be uphill. Typically, hangars (and other airport areas) are on relatively flat ground, but even a slight uphill in front of your hangar can be extremely frustrating. When I was a young pilot flying a Cherokee 6 owned by my first flight instructor, I vividly remember one night trying to get that aircraft into a hangar by myself—unsuccessfully. We affectionately dubbed the small hill in front of his hangar "Beekman's Hill" and regularly required assistance from a second person to push any of the heavier aircraft into the hangar. But alone that night after midnight, at a young 18 years old, I just didn't have the strength to get the aircraft into the hangar by myself.

In another instance at a friend's hangar, I found myself completely unable to put his Seneca away on an icy airport ramp, even with the help of a gas-powered tug. The tug even had chains on the wheels. Unable to get the airplane put away by myself, I had to place a rescue call to a local friend who fortunately was able to come and help. As these stories illustrate, a quick look for a hill (even one that is minimally perceptible) in front of a hangar could save you lots of difficult pushing and frustration at some point in the future.

. . .

The features and options discussed above are important to consider when selecting hangar storage. The next sections cover different types of actual hangar structures, their features, and the advantages and disadvantages of each.

Community Hangars

Some airports have large hangars that serve as homes for multiple aircraft often owned by different owners. In these cases, an aircraft owner typically rents space in a hangar, although it might not necessarily always be the same reserved space. This shared space is usually offered at a lower price per month than hangars that are dedicated to one specific aircraft, but community hangars do have some disadvantages.

I have seen various types of these hangars: big boxes, buildings with doors on two or three sides, and T-style nested buildings. No matter the physical structure, a key point is that there are no barriers between the bays in which individual aircraft park. Community hangars are more secure than an open ramp but not as secure as an individual hangar. In most cases, security is pretty reliable since people with access to the building are also typically aircraft owners.

When using a community hangar, your aircraft may not always be the one parked in the front. This means that getting your aircraft in or out of the hangar could require moving multiple other aircraft. The same will hold true for other hangar owners who will need to move your aircraft if it happens to be the one in front. In either case, it means more work moving aircraft around and more people potentially moving your aircraft more often, both in your presence and when you are not around.

If your aircraft is in a community hangar, it will be more likely to experience "hangar rash" damage as you or others move aircraft around to gain access. Wing tips, tails, and towbars attached to nose gears are common areas of concern. Even if your aircraft doesn't receive any damage, it can be easy to do damage to another tenant's aircraft as you move it around to gain access to your own. This may leave you liable for damage to other aircraft.

If you store your aircraft in a community hangar, it is less likely that you will also be able to store other things there. One benefit many hangar owners or renters take advantage of is the extra space available to them for storage of aviation or non-aviation items in addition to storing their aircraft. But in community hangars, it might not be possible to store even basic items such as wheel pants that have been removed from your aircraft, tools, extra cases of oil, or other supplies. Even if these items are allowed, a pilot may have concerns about the security of keeping them in a hangar shared by multiple operators.

If you will be using a community hangar, consider some of the potential disadvantages in relation to the benefits—the main one typically being lower cost. It may also be worth finding out if the other aircraft in a community hangar are really active or only occasionally used. Many aircraft owners fly very few hours each year, and a couple hangar queens tucked away in the back may only very rarely require repositioning, allowing your aircraft to be parked up front for easy in-and-out access.

FBO Hangar Rental

When larger FBOs are present at airports, they sometimes offer hangar space in their facilities. This commonly comes with in-and-out services where their staff will pull out and put away your aircraft.

While space in a large FBO hangar may be more costly, the services these hangars provide can be fantastic. Having trained and qualified staff moving your aircraft around for you can reduce the potential for damage, and if damage does occur, it puts the FBO on the hook for the costs.

Another benefit to hangaring with an FBO on the field relates to available maintenance services. In some cases, hangar tenants at FBOs are given maintenance discounts or priority. This can be valuable when things break. Fuel discounts are also common benefits. Security in these facilities is usually good since there is staff around to watch and check up on aircraft. It is rare that an unknown person will be able to gain access to an aircraft unchallenged.

However, there are potential negatives to hangaring with an FBO on the field. One is that, as is the case with community hangar space, it is unlikely that you will be able to store items other than your aircraft in an FBO hangar.

If the FBO operates charter service, provides fueling or tugging services to an airline on the field, or even services larger corporate aircraft, smaller GA aircraft owners may find that their aircraft take a backseat to the priorities of larger clients. When you are in a hurry to depart but the FBO has three airliners to fill with gas before the on-duty line staff can tug your aircraft out and fuel it, the delay may become frustrating. If you have time to kill or you can call ahead to have your aircraft pulled out for you, this may not be an issue. It can also be a potential problem if the FBO is not a 24-hour-a-day operation. If you need to leave early or late, or return after hours, getting your aircraft in or out of the hangar may be more difficult or come with a fee.

At some airports, it can also be hard to provide others with access to your airplane if you are not there. Do you have a friend you want to lend it to? Or perhaps you've arranged for a fellow pilot to fly your airplane to pick you up somewhere. If the airport or FBO only allows "badged" or approved people to get access to a plane, these situations may be more difficult or impossible, especially on short notice.

If an FBO hangar option is available at an airport you are considering, these are all questions to inquire about before signing an agreement for hangar services. Determine what benefits would come with the FBO hangar rental as well as any potential negatives before making a final decision.

T-Hangars and Box Hangars

The most common hangar options available at most airports are rental T-hangars or box hangars. Both are commonly developed by airport owners, municipalities, or independent developers on airport grounds in line formats with multiple hangars under one roof. Each hangar has its own doors and four closed walls (although some do not necessarily block off all internal walls), effectively giving each aircraft its own space.

Rates for these hangars vary widely based on the local market, but they are typically more expensive than other options except for building your own personal hangar. Most of these are constructed to standardized sizes that will fit most light, single- and twin-engine GA aircraft. However, it is worth noting that some older T-hangars and box hangars are not quite as wide and may have difficulty fitting modern aircraft that have longer wingspans, such as some Cirrus or Diamond aircraft.

Amenities in these hangars vary, but many have electricity and some have heat. If electricity and/or heat is available, make sure you know who is responsible for paying the bill. On a related note, if your hangar doesn't have heat but has electricity provided by the landlord, leaving a high-powered electrical heater on to keep your hangar warm through the winter will eventually get noticed. The landlord's electrical bill will increase significantly, and in one case I witnessed, it wasn't hard to figure out whose hangar was the culprit. It was the only one in the row of T-hangars that didn't have snow on the roof because it was so warm. Although the tenant did not get evicted, he did get a "bill adjustment."

One benefit of these types of hangars is that aircraft owners are typically able to store other things that relate to the use of their aircraft—such as tools, supplies, or other aircraft parts—as long as the primary use of the hangar is aircraft storage. Some hangar lease agreements even allow the space to be used for aircraft maintenance or permit pilots to put couches and other comfort items in their rented hangars. Many pilots have turned parts of their hangars into veritable pilot caves or flight planning areas that they use for preparation or just relaxing before or after flights. It isn't uncommon for a grill to appear from one of these hangars on a nice Saturday afternoon and for a few hangar tenants to congregate for brats or burgers as the sun goes down over the runway.

When renting a hangar, it is important to carefully read the hangar lease agreement to understand what is and what is not allowed within the use restrictions. It is worth noting that it is extremely rare for a hangar lease agreement to allow the storage of aircraft fuel. The dangers of storing large quantities of fuel (beyond the already significant number of gallons in the aircraft themselves) is generally considered to be an unnecessary fire risk. In addition, allowing tenants to store their own fuel can be detrimental to the local fuel provider's sales.

It is also common for grills and other flame-producing items to not be allowed inside hangars. Although grilling inside your hangar might sound good, all that 100LL in the aircraft's wings must be kept away from open flames or other ignition sources.

Most rented T-hangars and box hangars do not allow aircraft maintenance to be conducted inside. If you are looking to tinker a bit on your plane, this will likely be overlooked, but if you are hoping to have your A&P use the space to complete your annual or 100-hour inspections, this may be frowned upon or even be grounds for eviction. Pay attention to provisions in your rental agreement that prohibit or limit work being done in your rented hangar.

If you are considering storing other items in the hangar, understand what the rental agreement allows. Winter storage of your Porsche may be allowed in some places but not in others. Most hangars will allow storage of some extra items as long as the primary use of the facility remains aircraft storage. But if the hangar becomes filled with all the extra paperwork from your business and your kids' stuffed animals and toys, or if it otherwise begins looking like an abandoned storage unit that can no longer even fit an aircraft, someone will probably say something. Eviction may follow.

Larger Hangars

If you have a larger aircraft or multiple aircraft, it may be necessary to secure space in a larger hangar. Many airports have corporate-style hangars available for rent for larger or multiple aircraft. These are typically more costly but commonly have more amenities than single T-hangars or box hangars. Although they can be more expensive, they may in fact be more cost-effective than renting multiple, single-aircraft hangars.

Larger aircraft will obviously require larger hangars. At some locations, larger hangars are the only options for pilots who fly mid-sized, twin-engine aircraft or light jets. These hangars are also commonly set up for use by multiple aircraft. This can enable an owner to set up facilities that will allow all their support equipment for multiple aircraft to be in one building, eliminating the need to transfer equipment between multiple, single-use hangars.

Larger hangars will sometimes come with additional amenities. Many will include bathroom facilities, and some have office space in or attached to the side of the hangar. Others have garage ports or doors where you can store vehicles while out on flights. A few even contain conference rooms or sleep rooms. These hangars can almost become personal FBOs, offering stand-alone facilities that owners can set up to meet all of their aviation needs. These hangars are common targets for rental or development by companies with active business travelers who use their aircraft on a regular basis.

Building or Purchasing Your Own Hangar

Just as renting an apartment for your primary residence may not meet all your needs or wildest desires for a home, a rental hangar may be unable to fully meet all your needs for aircraft storage. If this is the case, building your own hangar may be in your future. This might also be the only option if you live in an area where hangar space is already spoken for (some places have long wait lists) or if no hangars exist (yes, some airports do not have hangars).

Building a hangar is a much larger commitment than using a shorter-term rental, but it can also provide you and your aircraft with a long-term base that is entirely your own and that you can make into exactly what you want.

Having a private, custom hangar gives you the opportunity to get exactly what you want and need. You can build (or buy) a hangar that will comfortably house one or multiple aircraft and that has amenities you might not find in rental hangars. It is not uncommon for private hangars to become elaborate "pilot caves" that serve both as places to store aircraft and as clubhouses.

Office space, sitting rooms, recreation rooms, bathrooms, bars, storage areas, and much more can be built into a custom, private hangar in addition to the floor space used for storing or maintaining an aircraft. If you are considering building a hangar, the sky may be the limit for what you can consider incorporating into the building.

While I won't go into every detail you should consider when thinking about building a hangar, there are a few worth noting that could make a difference in your choice to build or rent. Smaller decisions like which door to install, whether to install a separate door for a car, or what specific type of heating system to install will be part of the planning process if you decide to build your own hangar. But there are other, major considerations to evaluate that might make a difference in helping you determine if building or renting is right for you.

You should carefully evaluate what utilities are available at the site you are considering for your hangar. In many cases, hangars built on airports away from other infrastructure may require that new lines be run for utilities such as gas, electric service, or sewer. This work may end up being at the sole expense of the owner or developer, and the costs can add up very quickly. If any utilities will need to be added, get quotes on the potential costs for these developments before finalizing any agreements.

If you want a bathroom in your hangar but a sewer connection is not available, you may be able to build a septic system. But these are not allowed in some locations. If gas lines are not available near your hangar, you might be able to put a propane tank outside the hangar for fueling a heating system. However, this can get very expensive to run in cold winter climates. Therefore, it's important to evaluate the utilities. The proximity to available utilities services or the alternative options available may be a deciding factor in selecting an airport on which to build a hangar.

Some of the coolest features I have seen built into hangars include a bar area, a lounge area, doors that can be operated with "remote openers," and—my personal favorite—a heated apron in front of the doors. That particular example was built with in-floor heating that was extended to 30 feet in front of the hangar. Not only did we not need to shovel the snow in front of the building, but we also didn't have to worry about traction as we pulled the aircraft out or pushed it back into the hangar. No more slipping on an icy ramp for that particular owner! If you are planning to build a hangar, take the time to really figure out what you want before you finalize the details. Get quotes for the work and then consider everything together to help you determine your priorities of what you need, want, and perhaps can live without.

You should carefully consider the available options for owning or leasing the property for your hangar. Do your homework before making any decisions. At most publicly owned airports, unless you are purchasing land next to the airport grounds, you won't be able to "buy" the property on which you will place your hangar. It is typical to lease the ground for a period of time, either for an upfront, lump sum fee or based on a yearly lease. The cost of the lease is normally calculated based on a per-square-foot rate and includes use of the ground on which the hangar is built and potentially some adjacent land (for parking, easement, access, etc.) over the term of the contract.

There are a few things to watch out for when considering a ground lease for your hangar. The first thing to look at is the term of the lease. Make sure the term is sufficiently long to meet your needs (and make your investment in building the hangar worthwhile). An airport may offer different lengths of leases as options or sometimes only a predetermined, fixed-term lease. It is also common to have renewing lease terms for periods of time that can be extended through mutual acceptance by both the municipality and the ground lease holder.

Carefully consider any use restrictions present in a ground lease. Some leases restrict use of a hangar to only aircraft storage and may limit the use of a hangar for other business purposes, prohibit the conduct of maintenance inside a hangar, prohibit storage of non-aviation equipment or goods, or provide other limiting conditions. Most ground leases prohibit habitation of a hangar as a residence (although certainly this may be allowed in fly-in communities). While any particular restrictions might not be a problem for your use, it is also worth considering what effect those restrictions may have on your ability to resell the hangar at some point in the future.

For example, if you build a nice, big, corporate hangar for your own use and then try to sell it in 20 years when you retire, you might not be able to find another corporate buyer but might discover an interested maintenance provider. However, if conducting maintenance is prohibited in the hangar, you could lose the ability to make the sale.

You should also determine what the insurance requirements are for a building on the property. Most municipalities (or airport grounds owners) will have minimum insurance requirements for buildings and other facilities. Depending on the requirements, this can be a significant cost for a hangar owner. Frequently, the insurance will be required to include not only building coverage, but also coverage for more general "slip and fall" types of liabilities. An airport or its operator may also require that a hangar owner indemnify the municipality or other airport users as a part of the insurance coverage. Discuss with a credible insurance broker what options are available and at what price. It's a good idea to do this before you begin construction or possibly even before signing an agreement with an airport for a ground lease or sale of property. Know what insurance will be required, whether you can obtain the appropriate coverages, and at what cost they will be obtainable.

From the day you start thinking about building a hangar, you should be considering its resale. While you may be planning on owning the hangar for many years, life changes may make it necessary to sell your hangar at some point. The agreements you make when negotiating your ground lease will make a significant difference in resale value of the hangar and even can determine whether selling your hangar is possible at all.

In some cases, it can be very difficult to transfer a ground lease, so it's a good strategy to have the ground lease in the name of a corporation. To make any potential transfer of hangar ownership as easy as possible, the best method may be to set up a corporation that has no activity other than owning the building and holding the ground lease for the property on which the hangar sits. This allows for the transfer of the ownership of the company to effectively transfer ownership of the hangar, and it may circumvent municipal approval requirements for transfer of the hangar ownership (as long as the uses of the hangar still meet the provisions of the ground lease agreement).

It is not uncommon for lease agreements to include a clause stating that at the end of the term of the lease, the building will become the property of the municipality from which the ground is leased. If this is at the end of a 10-year term, it may not be worth the investment to build a hangar. If the term is 30 years, it may be more worthy of consideration. It is also possible that the lease terms can be renewed by any number of clauses in the contract, such as by auto-renewing or by mutual agreement of the two parties. Carefully consider these potential limitations in the lease agreement and how they could affect the use or potential resale of a hangar.

If suitable property is not available on the field for your hangar needs, you might consider property adjacent to the airport. If you are considering buying property next to the airport and using it to develop a hangar, first find out if the airport allows what is called "through the fence access" to the airport.

At many airports, building of taxi streets or other access from off-airport property is not allowed on airport grounds. Even if it is currently allowed, the rules and regulations could possibly change over time, so make sure you have a sufficiently long contract agreement for access if you are considering developing your hangar on property adjacent to the airport.

Most of the advice here probably seems focused on a case in which you are building a new hangar, but the same advice applies to purchasing an already-built hangar. The main difference is that in the latter case, you may not be able to change the covenants that affect the property. If you are considering purchasing someone else's hangar, find out the details of the ground lease, the use provisions, the renewal procedures, and if there are any outstanding concerns about the legal standing of the ground lease or building condition. And although it's probably a given, I'll add a reminder that you should get a good inspection of the building itself and its facilities.

In some locations, a middle ground exists between building and renting hangars. Much like in the home market, condos may be an option. In these cases, hangars are "purchased" as a condo and become owned by a specific individual. These units may or may not be attached to other similar condos. This option can offer a nice middle ground between building your own hangar and renting something that won't ever be yours. The terms can vary on these facilities, but they are worth considering if they are an option in your area.

If you plan to build or buy a hangar, it's worth taking your time and talking with lots of other people who have already done so. Find out about their experiences—what they liked, what they didn't like, and what they wish they had included in their hangars but didn't. Take good notes, incorporate their feedback, and plan carefully. Building a hangar is much like building a home. Personal taste will have a great effect on the final outcome.

Location, Location, Location

Whether you are renting or are building your own hangar, consider the location of the hangar on the field. It will not do you any good to have a hangar that requires taxiing between two buildings if your wings won't fit through the space. Take the time to evaluate the location and even try taxiing your aircraft to the hangar you are intending to use. In many cases, hangar rows are placed very close together, and getting an aircraft out of and back into a hangar may be a tight squeeze. Every year, insurance companies receive numerous claims for aircraft wing damage that occurs when owners bump into their hangars while taxiing.

The hangar's location on the field can also determine how much taxiing you will have to do and, if it's a towered airport, whether you will be likely to easily get clearances. Being the last hangar on the line sometimes means that other aircraft might block your way in or out of taxiways. It can be worth looking at the hangar's location in the winter if you live in a snowy area. Does where and how the airport plows the snow in any way inhibit where you will need to taxi your aircraft?

Vehicle parking and access can also be a factor to look at. Being able to drive to the hangar will allow for easy loading and unloading of luggage or supplies. The ability to park right at your hangar can help you avoid long walks to or from the car in the rain, which inevitably will come just after you put your aircraft away.

If you have a choice among multiple hangars on the field, think about which location will best serve your needs. South-facing hangars are more likely to have snow and ice melt off in front of them during the winter, while the same south-facing hangar may get overly warm in southern climates during the heat of summer. In some cases, perhaps the view is all that matters. Picking a hangar that faces west instead of east may be better since it will let you sit on your hangar couch and watch the sun set over the airport.

Or, you could consider social factors such as whether the hangar is near your friends. I have known lots of folks over the years who have built hangars next to their friends, and the airport became a gathering place for many of them and their fellow aviation aficionados on every sunny Saturday afternoon.

Chapter 7

Tugs and Towbars

It's important to have the right hangar in which to store your aircraft, as discussed in the previous chapter. But you also must be able to get your aircraft out of the hangar, and hopefully back into it after you fly, which can be a challenge without the right equipment. Basically, the bigger the aircraft, the more power, and perhaps the bigger the tug, will be needed to get it in and out of a hangar. A hand towbar may work great for the owner of a Cessna 152 in a T-hangar, but it probably won't do the trick for a Piper Aerostar owner who needs to pull the aircraft out of the hangar without help, especially on an icy ramp. A common oversight for many owners is not thinking through what method they will use to get their aircraft in and out of the hangar with minimal effort and risk. Yes, I said risk. If you do this the wrong way, you may hurt yourself or your aircraft—or both.

Factors to Consider

That hand towbar that is tucked away in the back or nose baggage area of your aircraft may be OK in a pinch, but most times that you move your aircraft, it probably won't do the job either easily or safely.

For some owners, the movement of an aircraft in and out of a hangar is a non-issue because this task is handled by a full-time FBO at the location where they operate. If this is the case for you, fantastic. But for most owners, moving their aircraft will require some level of personal involvement. For you, this means that when you want to operate your aircraft, you must have the means and the ability to move it.

When determining what will work best to get your aircraft in and out of a hangar, think about your physical capabilities. Naturally, bigger and stronger individuals may be able to more easily move certain aircraft than would a smaller person. This is simply a matter of physics. But that ability may also be diminished as we get older or encounter injuries that result in physical limitations, or it may be dependent on whether we are operating an aircraft solo or have friends or others available who can help.

In addition to considering your physical abilities, let's look at the different methods and equipment that could be used to move an aircraft in and out of a hangar and any risks associated with them.

Types of Tugging Equipment and Methods of Moving Aircraft

Human-Powered Towbars

Many light, general aviation aircraft are easily moved by a simple hand towbar attached to the nose wheel and pulled by the pilot, perhaps with a little help from the passengers. This method is probably the safest when it comes to potential damage to an aircraft. It's hard to pull an aircraft by hand with enough force to do much damage by running into a hangar door or overturning a nose wheel. But this method also requires the most physical work, and I've seen an aircraft's momentum get away from the operator and result in a "run-away."

If you are planning on pulling your aircraft in and out of the hangar by hand as a matter of normal operation, make sure you can manage the process in all conditions, not just on the best of days or once in a while using the maximum expenditure of your strength. If that isn't the case, then it's time to start considering something with a little horsepower of its own to help you out.

Powered Hand Tugs

One of the most common upgrades that owners invest in is a gas- or electric-powered hand tug. These are bigger versions of a hand towbar, powered by either a gas or electric engine. Offered in two-wheeled or single-wheeled options, these types of tugs basically take a hand towbar and add a wheel driven by a motor that serves as a method to get the aircraft moving. This takes the hard work off the pilot, only requiring that the pilot steer the tug to keep the aircraft moving.

There are two major styles of these motor-powered tugs: one attaches to the main wheel of the aircraft and the other has a pad that lifts the main wheel of the aircraft off the ground. Towbars that attach to the main wheel work for most light aircraft, but heavier aircraft may slip in wet or icy ramp conditions. With the towbars in which the main aircraft wheel rolls onto a pad that then moves, this allows the weight of the aircraft itself to push down on the tug wheels, which increases the traction maintained by the tug as it moves the aircraft.

When considering these motor-powered hand tugs, evaluate the weight of your aircraft using the maximum gross weight and determine if the tug's horsepower will be sufficient to handle the aircraft. If you have the option, try using the tug a couple of times. Underpowered tugs are more likely to slip, burn out motors, or result in difficulty when moving an aircraft in and out of a hangar.

These tugs do still require that the operator be physically capable of hooking them up, walking with them as the aircraft is moved, and turning the aircraft main wheel. If you think this will be beyond your physical abilities, then a riding type of tug may be required.

Don't be afraid to look for used models, and you may even consider one that someone tells you has a "shot motor." Tugs are typically very simple machines, and a broken tug often can be fixed very inexpensively. A common fix that gets many tugs back in working order is a simple carburetor overhaul. If you are mechanically inclined, you may choose to do this yourself. I have seen many tugs that were sold at rock bottom prices get fixed by small, local engine shops for pennies on the dollar compared to the purchase price of a brand-new tug.

There are numerous options for powered hand tugs on the market, so do a little homework before you buy one. There can be significant variations in price. The simpler the model, the less expensive they are. Prices will certainly be higher for larger or more powerful models. The decision about what to buy depends on the level of convenience you are willing to pay for. There are even several very cool, electric-motor-powered, remote-control options available if you are willing to spend the money on them!

Lawn Tractors with a Towbar

I am a big fan of small lawn tractors for moving mid-sized aircraft. Aircraft such as the Piper Navajo or the Cessna 400 series aircraft are great examples of planes that are quite heavy to move by hand, even with lighter, powered hand tugs, but which do not require a full-sized tug to get moving. In fact, a used lawnmower with the mowing deck removed can be a great option for these mid-sized aircraft and can often work for pilots on a tight budget.

Like with larger tugs, a towbar that can attach to the lawn tractor will be required, but many of these tractors have hitch points where a ball or hitch can be installed. In some cases, this can even be installed on the front of the lawn tractor to make it easier to see the aircraft when it is being pushed or pulled.

The main benefits of towing setups using lawn tractors are that they are affordable, offer the ability to control the vehicle movement to go very slowly, and are not powerful enough to do major damage to an aircraft quickly. As an added benefit, the weight of the operator sitting on the seat helps the wheels gain traction, and some wheels can be equipped with chains for winter operations.

Towbars on an Automobile or Tractor

Often, hitch-attached towbars can also be hooked up to trailer or hitch points on cars, trucks, or even larger full-sized tractors. I strongly advise caution here.

While the horsepower can be helpful for an aircraft that is hard to move either because of conditions or because of its weight, a passenger vehicle or a tractor provides much more power than is required to move most aircraft. In addition, the fact that the driver is inside the passenger compartment with their view restricted to some degree can increase the chance of the situation turning bad very quickly. Moving too rapidly, turning too sharply, or jerking the aircraft can quickly result in expensive or even catastrophic damage.

If you are going to use a towbar attached to an automobile or tractor, even if only on rare occasions, get a passenger or fellow pilot to watch what you are doing from the outside, and move very slowly. The faster you move, the more quickly damage can happen.

Purpose-Built Aircraft Tugs

While this is possibly the costliest option, some owners do end up purchasing a purpose-built aircraft tug. These don't always have to be purchased new, as FBOs, airports, or airlines often have used tugs for sale, or they may be available through auctions. These tugs can be great items for owners of larger aircraft.

The big benefit of a purpose-built aircraft tug is that the hookup for the towbar will typically be on the "front" of the tug—the direction that the driver is facing. Although this may seem like a small detail, looking at the towbar while facing forward significantly decreases the likelihood that the driver will overturn the nose wheel or jackknife the nose wheel or towbar in the process. It also allows the driver to look forward while pushing an aircraft backward into a hangar, improving the driver's ability to watch the wings and reducing the potential of striking the wings on the sides of the hangar. Trying to do this while looking back over your shoulder is always more difficult.

Purpose-built tugs come in a variety of sizes. In general, the bigger the tug, the bigger the aircraft it will be able to move. With that said, a tug that is oversized for the aircraft it is moving has the potential to more forcefully push the aircraft and cause damage. You don't need a surplus B-52 tug for your Beechcraft Sierra. Even if such a tug is a great deal, a little moderation is advised.

Specialty Towbars

Some aircraft are more easily moved with specialty towbar apparatus. Not every aircraft is tricycle gear!

If you are the owner of a tailwheel aircraft, you will probably find yourself in need of a towbar that attaches to the tail wheel of your aircraft. A hand towbar may suffice for lighter aircraft, but these may not be enough for heavier aircraft. In many hangars, aircraft are pulled in with the tail at the back of the hangar. With some tailwheel aircraft, this may not leave enough room to get a motorized vehicle behind the aircraft to hook up a towbar. In these cases, a motorized hand tug that lifts the tail wheel may be a good option.

Another option for some aircraft is to use a triangle-style, main gear towbar. These are used most commonly for larger tailwheel aircraft. The towbar is attached to the main wheels, allowing a vehicle connected to the towbar to move the aircraft from the front of the hangar. Although this is probably the least common type of towbar, if you are the owner of a North American T-6 or Mustang, it might just be the best option out there for your needs.

Safety and Damage Prevention

No matter what kind of towing apparatus you are using to move your aircraft, make sure the parking brake is off. When you are moving an aircraft by hand, leaving the brake on probably won't result in anything worse than some strained muscles and your failure to budge the aircraft. However, if you are trying to move the aircraft using something more powerful, it can result in major damage. Dragging an aircraft with the parking brake on can cause flat spots on the tires, and pulling on a nose wheel when the parking brake is locked on the main wheels can cause the collapse of the nose wheel. I know of a very expensive case in which an FBO tried to move a Piaggio Avanti while the parking brake was still on. The tug ended up collapsing the nose wheel and the damage climbed to well over $100,000 very quickly.

Regardless of what kind of towbar or machinery you are using to move your aircraft, pay attention to any turning limits there may be for the nose wheel of the aircraft. This is especially important on aircraft that do not have free-castering nose wheels; these often have visually depicted turning limits that you should remain within on each side during towing efforts. If you turn beyond this limit, especially when the aircraft is forced with too much power using a tug or vehicle to move it, serious damage can result.

Make sure that any towbar you use properly fits the attach points recommended by the manufacturer for movement of the aircraft. A towbar for a Cessna may not fit a Piper. Get the correct attach point for the specific airplane. If the aircraft is supposed to be towed by the tabs above the nose wheel, do not tow it using a tire attach point, and vice versa.

There is a reason that the manufacturer has set towing points, so use the recommended attach points and use a towbar that properly fits them. Using one that does not fit properly may result in the towbar slipping off and causing damage to the gear, cowling, or other parts of the aircraft.

Seasonal Conditions

Depending on where you base your aircraft, changing weather conditions can be a major factor in what you will need to get your aircraft in and out of a hangar in different seasons.

On many occasions, I have seen icy ramps that thwart even the best attempts of owners to get their aircraft out of—and especially back into—their hangars. In at least two instances, these efforts resulted in injuries requiring the owners to make a trip to the hospital. Both were the result of the owners slipping and falling on the ice as they tried to pull their aircraft out of a hangar. One of the owners hurt his back, and the other hit his head on the pavement, resulting in a concussion and some stitches. I know this may sound overdramatic, but I have heard many other stories of these types of incidents that result in lesser but still painful injuries.

If you are trying to move an aircraft in and out of a hangar by hand on an icy surface, I strongly encourage the use of shoe-bottom spikes, which are readily available from outdoor equipment suppliers. These spikes add some traction and are a regular part of my winter flying kit.

A more permanent solution is to consider one of the motorized options described above. But even if you use one of those, some modifications may be required for winter operations. You might be thinking, how can I justify spending $1,000, $2,000, or more on a tug? The answer is, easily. How much might you spend in medical bills if you hurt yourself instead of investing in a tug?

When you are considering the purchase of any type of tug, it can be helpful to evaluate if the tires can be equipped with chains or studded tires for winter use. Having chains or studs on tires can allow a tug to get a better bite on slippery ramps and could make the difference between slipping tires that don't go anywhere and actually getting the aircraft moving.

If you don't have the ability to add chains or studded tires, having a bag of sand available can help. By spreading some sand in the track where your tug wheels will be traveling, it can sometimes provide enough grip to get things moving even without chains or studs.

I strongly advise against using salt, even though many people commonly use it on their home sidewalks or driveways. For the thin aluminum of aircraft, salt can become quickly corrosive and cause damage. I have seen some owners use kitty litter for traction, but I personally have found that its water absorption properties can result in formation of a soggy, muddy mess on the ramp in front of the hangar. The easiest, cheapest, and least messy option in the long run is probably just some simple dirt.

Remember to Remove the Towbar

I am sure you can imagine how much damage is done when a pilot forgets to remove the towbar from an aircraft before starting it and taxiing away—or worse, taking off. I would be remiss not to mention this here. Some of the insurance underwriters I know have told me it is a significant percentage of the claims they get every year for damage. These occurrences don't always end up in accident or incident reports with the FAA or NTSB because the towbars usually get noticed before takeoff. But sometimes pilots actually take off with towbars still attached, and this can end up in major aircraft damage and potentially life-threatening situations.

The majority of these cases are less likely to cause injury to the pilot, but they commonly cause damage to the aircraft. A forgotten towbar on a single-engine aircraft will regularly cause the propeller to strike it. This might not occur immediately during startup, but the bouncing a towbar may experience during taxiing often will cause it to contact the propeller. When this happens, the resulting damage to the propeller and any stoppage of the engine may require that the pilot "tear down" some engine components. The resulting bill can climb quickly because of a simple oversight that could have easily been avoided.

In multi-engine aircraft, propellers will be less likely to strike a towbar on the nose wheel, but a towbar can easily do damage to the gear if it hits cracks in the pavement while the aircraft is taxiing or during turns.

If a pilot does get to the point of takeoff, the swinging towbar attached to the aircraft will likely cause damage in the air, can become jammed during landing and cause more damage, and will obviously be problematic if the aircraft has retractable gear and the pilot attempts to retract the gear with the towbar attached. I know of several accidents that ended up in total aircraft losses because the pilots forgot to unattach a towbar prior to flight.

So remember to remove your towbar! It's probably less likely that you will miss a motor-powered hand tug attached to the nose of your aircraft prior to start or taxi, but hand towbars and towbars attached to tugs or other vehicles commonly get forgotten during hasty departure procedures if the pilot leaves that job to another person and assumes it was done. In some aircraft, visibility of the towbar is limited from the pilot's seat, so it can easily get missed. Before you leave, either make sure you can see the towbar in the location it was placed after being removed from your aircraft or do one last outside walk-around of the aircraft to confirm that it is no longer attached.

Chapter 8

Maintaining Your Aircraft

As an aircraft owner, you will need to maintain your aircraft to keep it flying safely and reliably. This is a simple fact about aircraft. Parts break, things need servicing, and preventative maintenance is required to keep an aircraft operating properly. Many owner pilots are only minimally involved in the maintenance efforts associated with their aircraft, choosing to just trust their mechanic to tell them what they need to do. I think this is a mistake that can cost an owner more than it should and can potentially lead to unsafe operation of the aircraft.

Get to know your aircraft, understand what it needs to be maintained properly, and then select and work with a properly qualified mechanic who is familiar with your aircraft so you can get the best possible service and minimize aircraft downtime due to maintenance failures. Good maintenance for your aircraft is not only about ensuring you have a safe aircraft to fly, it is also about maximizing your aircraft's time in service so you can actually fly it when you want. A broken airplane doesn't do an owner much good.

With that in mind, let's start by talking about the requirements owners must comply with in order to be able to legally fly their aircraft.

Required Documents

During their training, most pilots learn some sort of acronym or mnemonic to help them memorize the documents that are required to be present in an aircraft for it to be legally operated. For many pilots, the last checkride they took was the last time they looked for these documents. It is an owner's job to make sure that these documents are available in the aircraft and are properly displayed when required in order for the aircraft to be operating within compliance with FAA regulations.

Let's start with the typical mnemonic used to help build a checklist of the documents that are required to be on board the aircraft. Many instructors use the acronym "SPARROW," which represents the following requirements:

S — Supplements
P — Placards
A — Airworthiness Certificate
R — Registration
R — Radio Station Certificate
O — Owner's Manual/Pilot's Operating Handbook
W — Weight and Balance

Let's briefly cover what each of these means for an owner.

Supplements

This refers to any supplemental documentation that must be kept in an aircraft that varies from the original owner's manual and the original equipment documentation provided by the manufacturers. It is becoming common for owners to be required to keep an increasing number of documents in their aircraft as they install new avionics systems, upgrade their aircraft with performance modifications, or add new equipment. Each of these additions and modifications may include different operation limitations or instructions that the equipment manufacturers require be carried on board the aircraft when it is operated. When an aircraft has had multiple modifications and upgrades, this can add up to a pile of additional manuals and limitations books that must all be carried in the aircraft!

Placards

Although these commonly become an afterthought, placards in the cockpit of the aircraft must be maintained and visible when required. The information on a placard can be as simple as a notation for where to have a hand hold in the aircraft for entry and exit or as complex as operating limitations for gear speeds or other aircraft systems. Required placards will be listed in the owner's manuals, pilot's operating handbooks, and/or supplemental documents that are required. As an owner, make sure that these placards are kept up and are visible for proper operating compliance.

Airworthiness Certificate

A legible airworthiness certificate is required to be in the aircraft and visible to any occupant within the cabin of the aircraft. The location that a pilot places the airworthiness certificate can vary from an entry door frame to a bulkhead in the back of the aircraft. This is a matter of preference for the owner, but no matter where it is placed, it must be visible and cannot be covered by other documents. Many owners have a "pouch" of some sort that they use to hold this and other documents. While it's a small technicality, make sure that this document is facing outward and that other documents are not covering or obstructing it. If the airworthiness certificate is not visible, a ramp check by an FAA official will probably note the lack of compliance.

Registration

Registration requirements may include both federal and state registrations. Regarding the state registration, I encourage owners to seek out their individual state's requirements. To meet federal requirements, the FAA requires that an owner register and renew the registration for an aircraft at least every three calendar years. This registration will obviously need to be updated if a change of ownership takes place. Even if there is no ownership change, the registration still must be kept current and kept in the aircraft when it is operated. You can learn more about the FAA aircraft registration process on the FAA's website. (Refer to this book's online Reader Resources at www.asa2fly.com/reader/avown.)

Radio Station Certificate

While there is no additional requirement for a pilot or aircraft operating in the United States, a pilot who operates internationally is required to hold a restricted radiotelephone operator permit issued by the Federal Communications Commission (FCC), and the aircraft is required to have a radio station license. If you will only be flying in the United States, you can ignore this requirement. However, if you are planning on flying outside of the United States, you should expect that the aircraft will need to have an FCC-issued "Radio Station License" and the pilot will need to have an FCC-issued restricted radiotelephone operator permit.

For the purposes of utilizing radios when flying internationally, each aircraft is considered a "station" and, as such, must have a license issued to it as a broadcasting facility. Visit the FCC's website for more information about this requirement and details on how you can apply for this license for your aircraft. (The direct links to this information are also available on this book's Reader Resources webpage at www.asa2fly.com/reader/avown.)

Owner's Manual/Pilot's Operating Handbook

Most aircraft were delivered with some sort of owner's manual or pilot's operating handbook that describes the limitations and operating guidelines under which an aircraft will be operated. The length and content of these documents varies depending on the manufacturer or the age of the aircraft, but even the sparsest of these documents must be kept in the aircraft when it is operated. Some of these manuals and handbooks are broader in their content while others are highly specific to the particular make and model of aircraft—or sometimes even the specific registration number of the aircraft. Make sure you have the correct one in the aircraft before you fly.

Weight and Balance

Last, but not least, a current weight and balance must be carried in the aircraft. This is the document that is used to compare with any weight and balance chart or operating requirements in the operating manuals, and it must be current and representative of the configuration of the aircraft. In some cases, owners choose to have multiple weight and balance documents certified to allow for options such as removing some seats to increase payload carriage.

I will cover this in more detail in Chapter 16, Modifying Your Aircraft to Enhance Performance.

. . .

I encourage owners to make copies of all of these documents and keep them in a safe place. If one of these documents becomes damaged or lost, a copy may suffice in a pinch until the original can be replaced.

Assuming that you have all of these documents in the aircraft and they are current, let's move on to talking about the required inspections that must be completed to keep your aircraft maintained properly.

Required Inspections

Another acronym that you might find helpful as an aircraft owner pertains to required inspections. You may already be familiar with it: the "AVIATE" acronym is commonly used to help a pilot remember and review the list of required inspections. I add an extra "A" to the front (A-AVIATE), and the letters represent the following inspection requirements:

A — Airworthiness Directives (ADs)
A — Annual Inspection
V — VOR (and GPS)
I — 100-hour Inspection
A — Altimeter Inspection
T — Transponder Inspection
E — ELT Inspection

Airworthiness Directives (ADs)

Commonly thought of as being similar to "recall" items for cars, airworthiness directives (ADs) are manufacturer-issued and/or FAA-issued inspections or changes to an aircraft that have been identified as needing service or replacement due to a safety concern for safe operation of flight. ADs may be one-time changes, requirements for ongoing monitoring, or major changes that stop an aircraft from being able to be operated until a change is made. The severity and the applicability of the inspection requirements is dependent on the potential danger posed by continued operation. ADs are not issued only on the airframe but may also be issued for components such as engines, propellers, avionics systems, brakes, or any other installed items in an aircraft. Compliance with ADs is mandatory for operating an aircraft in adherence with regulations.

Similarly, service bulletins (SBs) may also be issued by a manufacturer and address changes or inspections that have been recommended to more safely operate an aircraft or component. However, unlike ADs, compliance with SBs is not mandatory for private aircraft operations.

Some ADs can be highly onerous in the methods they require for compliance. In the worst cases, they can require frequent inspections of components that will surely need to be managed at more frequent intervals than the typical yearly annual inspections. The inspections might be required on an hourly basis; for example, two very common AD inspection requirements for numerous aircraft are an inspection of the exhaust system for cracks every 50 hours of operation and an inspection of seat track rails every 100 hours of operation. If you personally fly your aircraft 300 hours a year, you will need to plan to have your aircraft to a mechanic multiple times a year between the annual inspections to remain in compliance with ADs such as these. Every make and model of aircraft is a little bit different, and some have more ADs than others. Take the time to understand what is applicable to your aircraft and its systems. A savvy owner working with a good mechanic will have a good tracking system to ensure compliance with all applicable ADs.

Annual Inspection

Most owners know that their aircraft will need to have an annual inspection. This is the most basic inspection that is required to comply with general operating requirements. An annual inspection is required to be completed every 12 calendar months; this is defined as extending from the month in which it was last completed to the last day of the same month in the following year. Plan ahead to have the annual inspection completed before it expires to ensure you can keep operating your aircraft.

VOR (and GPS)

This check has been expanded over time to become more of an inspection of avionics navigation equipment and is primarily related to operation in IFR conditions. If you have a 1947 Stinson with no navigation equipment, you can skip this requirement. But if you plan to operate in IFR conditions, 14 CFR §91.171 contains a pilot regulatory requirement for a VOR equipment check for IFR operations. This check must have been completed within prescribed tolerances within the last 30 days to remain in compliance with operation requirements. If you can't remember how to do all the possible VOR checks and want to freshen up your knowledge on the topic, ASA's *Learn to Fly* blog article, "CFI Brief: Checking the accuracy of your VOR," provides more details about how to actually conduct VOR checks. (See the Reader Resources webpage at www.asa2fly.com/reader/avown.)

As many owners have expanded their aircraft's navigation equipment to include GPS navigation, they now must also ensure that their GPS equipment that is IFR-certificated has a current navigation database. These databases are updated every 28 days and must be uploaded into the aircraft's GPS system to be able to use the aircraft for IFR operations. Most systems display a database expiration date when they start up. The pilot can review this date and, if the date has not passed, determine that this GPS data can be used for navigation and approach operations. If the database has expired, it must be updated or else it is not authorized for use.

100-Hour Inspection

If the aircraft is operated for hire (for example, if flight training is being conducted in the aircraft for revenue), 100-hour inspections must be completed if more than 100 hours of flight takes place between the annual inspections. The best way to consider if this is applicable is to think about if "the aircraft" is generating revenue. If the aircraft is being rented to operators, this is probably the case and this inspection will be required. The 100-hour inspection is almost identical to an annual inspection, with one exception: an annual inspection must be completed by a mechanic with an

FAA Inspection Authorization (IA) certification, while a 100-hour inspection may be completed by an FAA-certificated Airframe and Powerplant (A&P) mechanic, which is a lower certificate level.

Altimeter Inspection

The FAA requires in 14 CFR §91.413 that equipment used for ATC transponder and altitude reporting be checked every 24 calendar months if it is to be used. This inspection requires that altitude reporting equipment is checked and is within prescribed tolerances to ensure that any reporting of altitude for ATC will be accurate. Additionally, the altitude system check, which is essentially a full pitot-static system check, will ensure that the altimeter system is accurately reflecting the proper altitudes, both depicted on the altimeter in the cockpit for the pilot and reported by the transponder system. This can certainly be helpful to a VFR flight operation, but it is obviously critical for IFR flight operations in which a pilot would not be able to determine relative altitude simply by looking out the window.

Transponder Inspection

The transponder is typically checked at the same time as the altimeter inspection for most IFR aircraft. This inspection is required under 14 CFR §91.413 along with being related to usage requirements under 14 CFR §91.215. However, in some cases this inspection is not done at the same time if a new transponder is required or, more commonly, in VFR-only-operated aircraft that have a transponder that is used for flight into airspace that requires transponder equipment.

It's worth noting that some owners have skipped these transponder inspections when they are only operating in VFR conditions, but if owners do this and they have a transponder in the aircraft, they are technically not allowed to use the transponder. The FAA doesn't indicate that a transponder must be inspected just for use in IFR conditions, but the regulation in fact indicates that "each person **operating** an aircraft equipped with an operable ATC transponder maintained in accordance with 14 CFR §91.413" [emphasis added] must have had the transponder inspected within the preceding 24 calendar months. So, according to the regulations, if you are going to use the transponder, it must have been inspected within the preceding 24 calendar months.

ELT Inspection

Finally, the emergency locator transmitter (ELT) must be checked and maintained within the battery compliance requirements found under 14 CFR §91.207. This ensures that if a pilot experiences an event such as a crash, the ELT will work properly, increasing the chances of that pilot being found in a timely manner.

• • •

Now that we have reviewed the list of required inspections that must be completed, let's look in detail at how owners can best ensure their aircraft receive the proper maintenance for efficient, reliable, and safe operation. An important part of this starts with finding the right maintenance provider for your aircraft.

Finding the "Right" Maintenance Provider

The mechanic located on the field where you keep your aircraft might not always be the best one to perform maintenance on your aircraft. If the mechanic is good, knows your aircraft, and you like them, then it could end up being a great choice. But it could be to your advantage to shop around a little bit to ensure you find the maintenance provider that will provide the best service for your specific aircraft.

Even if the mechanic at your home airport is great, they might not necessarily be familiar or experienced with your particular aircraft. If your local mechanic works primarily on single-engine Cessna and Piper legacy aircraft, they might not be the best choice to work on your aircraft if it's a Mitsubishi MU-2.

Take the time to talk with a few different mechanics and determine their knowledge level about your particular aircraft and its components. A mechanic that works primarily on Lycoming engines will likely not be the best one to work on your Continental engine, and vice versa. A truly good mechanic will tell you if they are not comfortable working on your aircraft and might even refer you to someone who is a more appropriate provider. When I owned an FBO that provided maintenance services, I expected my mechanics to do exactly that. In some cases, that honesty got me a dedicated customer at a later date after an owner sold one aircraft and purchased another for which our staff was more appropriately experienced.

References can also be an important thing to consider. Talk with other owners who have had maintenance provided by a mechanic or shop you are considering. There are many factors you can ask about in addition to pricing, such as did the mechanic communicate well with the client, was work completed in a timely manner, was the aircraft returned clean (instead of with grease all over the interior), were estimates provided before the work, and was the final price reasonable for the work completed? Another important consideration to ask about is how well the mechanic documented the work that was completed. Not all mechanics are great at "doing the paperwork," but that paperwork in the logbooks is what will document the work they performed. This can have a big impact on future maintenance work or sales efforts for the aircraft. Scribbled logbook entries that just list something like "annual inspection completed" will no longer cut it. A good professional mechanic will need to spend a significant amount of time properly documenting their work and putting that documentation into the maintenance records for the aircraft.

Depending on what aircraft you own, you may find mechanics that specialize in maintenance for the manufacturer or even the model of your aircraft. In some cases, it can be worth traveling some distance to have your regular maintenance completed. If you find a maintenance shop that specializes in Beechcraft aircraft like yours, it might be worth flying a few hundred miles to use that shop for your annual inspections or aircraft upgrades work rather than having it done by your local mechanic who only works on a Beechcraft every couple of years. This does not mean that the local mechanic won't be able to swap an alternator or change a brake if it goes out at your home airport, but for the long run, a shop that works frequently on your make and model of aircraft will know more of the common maintenance intricacies to look for in inspections and will be more likely to be aware of available options for improving your aircraft's dispatch reliability. Great sources for finding maintenance providers that specialize in your particular aircraft include aircraft type clubs, forums, or social media groups. Reach out to members of these groups and ask for recommendations, and then interview specific maintenance providers before scheduling that next maintenance.

I cannot stress enough how important it is to get quality maintenance. The cheapest mechanic you can find to sign off your aircraft after providing an annual on a Saturday afternoon in your hangar with a box of tools from his pickup truck will not be a good long-term solution. I have seen owners seek to "get the cheapest annuals" done year after year but then find that issues with their aircraft are missed, skipped, or purposely omitted from the maintenance work. Do you think the guy who is doing the annual in his free three hours on a holiday weekend is going to have an extra cowl clip available in his "parts store" in the back of his truck? Do you think he will go through the effort to order one and come back just to change that? Probably not. He will rig up the one that is there to "get it through 'til next year." This hodgepodge approach to maintenance breeds complacency, and over time, it will significantly affect the quality and safety of the aircraft. Do it right.

However, this doesn't mean that you can't have a mechanic complete maintenance in your hangar. Depending on airport operating and/or hangar rental agreements, you sometimes may be allowed to have a maintenance provider come to your hangar to do an annual instead of taking the aircraft to another location. A number of my clients have nice, heated, well-equipped hangars containing all the needed tools—in a few cases, even jacks for the aircraft—available for a mechanic to come in and complete the maintenance on their aircraft. This work often can take multiple days, and the owners pay a little premium for the mechanic to come to them, but in the end, they get fantastic maintenance service. It's important to evaluate what it will take to get the best maintenance for your aircraft at a reasonable price.

I would be remiss if I didn't also discuss pricing. As a general rule, "the cheapest" won't be the best, but the "most expensive" won't necessarily be the best either. Expect to pay a fair price considering market conditions. There is nothing inappropriate about calling several shops and asking for a quote on a base price for an annual or finding out their hourly shop rates for work on an aircraft to get a feel for the market. With a little information, you can determine if the maintenance provider you have selected is charging a comparable price within the market.

Some maintenance relationships go bad over time. I have witnessed many owners and maintenance shops become cross with each other over the years. In most cases, this situation develops because of poor communication about expectations by either or both of the parties involved. A mechanic who doesn't call the client before making a multi-thousand-dollar fix is likely to end up with an unhappy client. If a client finds a dead battery in their aircraft, asks a mechanic to install a new one, but doesn't ask the mechanic to also check if the alternator is properly charging, the client may be mad at the mechanic when the battery dies again. But the outcome could have been different if the owner had asked the mechanic to actually find and solve the problem instead of just change the battery. In these relationships, communication is key and is the mark of a good mechanic. I encourage owners to meet with their mechanics midway through service, after inspections are completed, to discuss any recommendations the mechanics may have for further service or needed repairs. There will likely be some "required" maintenance items that are related to airworthiness of the aircraft, but there might also be additional items that are preventative or elective in nature, which could be completed either during the current or at a future annual inspection, depending on the decisions of the owner.

If your relationship with your maintenance provider is going poorly, stop work. Do not make it worse. Schedule a meeting and communicate. Consider getting a second opinion. If a resolution is not possible, find alternative service providers. If this leaves your aircraft in the middle of maintenance being completed, be ready to get a special flight permit to ferry the aircraft to another provider, have the current maintenance provider put the aircraft together and bill you for work completed to date, or in the worst of cases, even move the aircraft via trailer to another shop.

Hopefully, you will never have to experience these challenges, but if you do, be reasonable and try to keep emotion out of it. It can be an expensive lesson to learn. By ensuring good communication ahead of time, asking for estimates and quotes, and having discussions during the time work is being completed, most disagreements can be avoided altogether or resolved by finding a middle-ground solution.

To some degree, an owner can make it easier for a maintenance service provider to deliver quality service. You can significantly increase the quality of maintenance and reduce the time it takes to complete by providing the service provider with proper documentation, allowing maintenance to be scheduled ahead of time for items that are not the result of unexpected failures, and having your aircraft physically available to provide the maintenance.

Another way to make your mechanic's job easier is to have the logbooks for the aircraft well organized. Most aircraft will have a combination of airframe, engine, and propeller logbooks that need to be maintained, updated, and consulted when maintenance is conducted. Additional documentation will probably include tracking of airworthiness directives (ADs) and/or service bulletins (SBs) indicating when or if they were required to be complied with, if they are one-time or recurring, and when they might need additional attention. Many owners leave this effort to their mechanics to deal with, but I encourage owners to get involved in tracking these items to avoid flying beyond their compliance. Some ADs are based on the number of hours of aircraft operation, not calendar time, and these hours can easily be overflown between annual inspections. A savvy owner that tracks the aircraft's hours of operation and the requirements for when ADs are due will be less likely to be out of compliance with AD service or inspection requirements between annual inspections.

Equipment That Frequently Breaks or Needs Replacement

Parts and components will break on your aircraft. It is a good idea to be aware of the common wear items that will need replacement over time and to budget for their replacement.

Following are some of the most common things that need to be regularly replaced on aircraft:

- Brakes
- Tires
- Vacuum pumps
- Batteries
- Heading indicators
- Attitude indicators
- Alternators/generators
- Starters

Some of these are obvious wear items on an aircraft, and it may even be worth having replacement parts available for when you need them. Brake pads and an extra set of tires certainly fall into this category for many owners.

In the case of other components, such as instruments, it may be more expensive to keep extra replacements on the shelf, but it is generally a good idea to be prepared to replace anything that has moving parts with new or overhauled instruments. For aircraft with vacuum systems, those vacuum instruments will not last forever. Over time, gyros fail and so do the pumps that drive them. In my own experience, it seems that most last for somewhere between 800–1,200 hours of flight before they need servicing. That servicing could involve removing and sending them in for overhaul, during which time the aircraft might not be flyable; swapping them with overhauled units; or buying and installing new replacements. With more modern avionics available, when older instruments fail many owners are choosing to install new, non-vacuum-driven instruments that fail less frequently. The factors that owners should take into consideration when making a decision are covered in more detail in Chapter 17: Avionics Upgrades.

Starters, alternators, and generators also are items that frequently fail. The obvious wear that these items take on a regular basis makes it easy to understand why they don't last forever. Keep these components in mind as you plan for future maintenance needs.

Following are some of the less obvious replacement items that owners sometimes choose to keep around:

- Selector knobs for radios—they tend to crack and break over time.
- Tailwheel springs—these seem to shimmy off on rougher ground and often can never be found again.
- Vortex generators (VGs)—it's useful to have a few extras in case any get knocked off and need replacing.
- Panel lights—for in-panel lighting posts; these tend to fail over time or get bumped and broken.

Although these tend to be more convenience items, they can be annoyingly difficult to find if lost or broken, and it may be a good idea to have a few extras on hand.

Tracking Aircraft Maintenance

Having a good method or system for tracking aircraft maintenance will help you understand what required maintenance is needed, what has been completed, and what might be coming up in the near future.

An owner can do this with varying degrees of complexity. It might be as simple as keeping maintenance logbooks and having a whiteboard on the hangar wall that lists when the next inspections are due, or it might get as complex as using aircraft dispatch and maintenance tracking software into which the owner enters all flights and maintenance requirements. Whichever method you choose, the more detail you include in your maintenance tracking, the better you will be able to track costs as well as predict and avoid overlooking any required maintenance service.

Most commercial operators—including those with charter, large corporate, and flight training aircraft—have maintenance tracking systems that dispatch an aircraft and include important notations about whether the aircraft is in compliance or is approaching any needed inspections. A private aircraft owner can simulate a personal version of this information very easily with tools available in our modern digital age. A Google Sheet or a Microsoft Excel spreadsheet can be a great tool to accomplish this, offering a low-cost middle ground for tracking personal aircraft maintenance and operations.

I have built Google Sheets documents for my own aircraft and for many owners with whom I fly. Users enter all their flights and the corresponding tachometer and/or Hobbs times, and then these times are automatically compared using formulas to entries showing the time since maintenance was last completed, when ADs are due, or when oil changes are desired. With a little spreadsheet work and as long as all the pilots use the tool, aircraft maintenance can be accurately tracked and pilots can avoid overflying any maintenance requirements. These sheets are shared with all operators of the aircraft and can be accessed easily through computers or tablet devices. These documents have become the flight tracking system we use for all of the aircraft that we operate. This method keeps us all on the same page as to each aircraft's maintenance history and upcoming needs.

Even simply keeping a notebook in the aircraft of flights flown and the corresponding times can provide operators of the aircraft with a tool to help keep maintenance on track. When a single pilot-owner is the sole operator of the aircraft, the complexity of operations tracking may need to be less detailed. When an aircraft is operated by partners, by members of a club, or by multiple pilots, using a more detailed and active tracking system becomes more important in order to coordinate between users.

It's essential that you at least use some method to track maintenance. No matter what system you choose, build one that will work for your use. Track as much information as you can. Record the aircraft's main inspections, but also document AD due dates, oil change due dates, VOR checks, GPS updates, etc. I think this gives you the basic idea. Don't just depend on the logbooks to help you track all of your maintenance needs and keep you in compliance with requirements before the next annual.

In later chapters, I will discuss repairs that owners may be able to complete on their own aircraft, FAA-approved "preventative" maintenance, how to determine if items are not working, whether a pilot is allowed to fly an aircraft taking into consideration the minimum equipment list (MEL), and other methods of determining if an aircraft is allowed to be operated with inoperative equipment.

With all of this in mind, following are a few pro tips that will be helpful for owners.

Pro Tips for Preventative and General Maintenance

- **Are you doing your own oil change?** Have a quick drain installed at the low point in the oil lines to allow you to easily hook up a funnel or hose to drain the oil. On many aircraft, if this is done correctly it can allow an oil change to be completed with minimal or no removal of cowlings.

- **Oil filter removal**—Removing the oil filter can be messy, especially for filters installed upside down on the top of the engine. Whether upside down or with the hole facing up, oil filters are notorious for being inconveniently placed in many aircraft and this can result in spilling of oil when they are removed. To minimize this, first drain the oil from the system. Then drain the filter. If the hole is facing up, a pro tip is to poke a hole in it and have a catch basin or bag underneath to catch the oil from the filter. If the filter is upside down (the hole facing down), poking a hole in it will provide airflow and the oil will drain into the oil system. In both cases, most of the oil will come out of the filter and leave less to spill when you remove it. After most of the oil is out of the filter, cover it with a ziplock bag or other plastic bag to catch any excess oil that might spill as you remove and replace it.

- **Tightening oil caps and filters**—All that is needed is finger-tight on oil caps, and hand-tight and perhaps just slightly snugger using an oil filter wrench on oil filters. An oil filter will have safety wire to keep it from spinning, and neither the oil cap nor filter will come off when they are snug but not overly tight. However, both can be *very* hard to get back off if you tighten them too much. An oil filter strap wrench and an oil cap wrench can be great tools to have in your box in case this happens.

- **Schedule the annual for your benefit**—Many owners schedule their annuals at specific times either to take advantage of "the 13th month" or so the inspections occur during periods of the year when the aircraft are not being actively used. If you own an open cockpit biplane, it probably will not get much use in northern Minnesota in January, so that might be a great time to have the aircraft down for maintenance. That would certainly be better than mid-June when you want to fly it to the local fly-in you go to every year. It can also be advantageous to schedule the annual so it is completed on the first day of a month. Annual inspections must be completed every 12 calendar months (defined as extending from any day of a month to the last day of the same month the following year). If you deliver your aircraft to a mechanic on the 25th of the month so it can be returned to you on the 1st of the next month, that effectively gives you 13 months of compliance instead of 12. The only challenge this approach causes for some owners is that every year, it shifts the month that the annual is due by one month, which can lead to some tracking challenges if the owner is not paying attention and documenting maintenance well.

- **Post-flight inspections**—Owners typically do pre-flight inspections, but post-flight inspections can be just as important. Would you rather find a problem with your aircraft as you put it away in your hangar, giving you time to fix it before you need to fly again, or discover the problem at 6:00 a.m. when you are trying to get on your way to an important business meeting or at 5:00 p.m. on Friday afternoon when you are planning to head out with your family for a weekend getaway? When you are putting the aircraft away, take the time to check for fluid leaks, check tires pressures and oil levels, and examine the airplane for other common issues or things that break. Getting in the habit of doing a thorough, post-flight inspection can minimize your frustration later.

• • •

Although there are lots of additional tips that can be helpful to aircraft owners, hopefully you will find the information in this chapter useful as you consider the maintenance of your aircraft. With the guidelines presented here, some forethought, a little planning, and dedication to details, you can effectively source and provide maintenance for your aircraft to keep it flying safely and efficiently for a long time.

Chapter 9

Documents You Should Own for Your Aircraft: Maintenance and Parts Manuals

Many owners count on their maintenance provider to have any documents needed for their aircraft beyond the pilot's operating handbook (POH). However, I encourage most owners to go beyond the basic POH and collect additional documents that can allow them to better understand their aircraft, help locate parts when necessary, and in some cases improve the quality of the maintenance that is provided.

Maintenance shops will not always have the service and parts manuals for every aircraft. Many shops will have the manuals for common aircraft, but if you have a make and model that is a little less common, having your own copies of manuals and supplying them to your maintenance provider can equip the provider with better information about your aircraft as they conduct maintenance.

In addition to the POH and aircraft/engine maintenance logs, I recommend that owners have the following three, additional, major sets of documents:

- Copies of applicable airworthiness directives (ADs)
- Aircraft, engine, and propeller parts manuals
- Aircraft, engine, and propeller service manuals

These documents will allow an owner as well as maintenance providers to better understand the manufacturer's recommended servicing procedures. The documents often provide inspection checklists for such things as 100-hour and annual inspections and include lists of approved parts and part numbers for aircraft components. Without these documents, the process can become a guessing game or require a lot of searching to find correct parts information. This can cause problems as it takes much more time and can result in installation of incorrect parts or maintenance work that is incomplete or incorrect.

An owner can easily source these documents with a little searching and minimal fees. There are a few common places from which you can obtain them:

- The manufacturer—These documents can commonly be obtained from the manufacturer (if it is still in operation), especially for more modern aircraft.
- Type clubs—Many type clubs offer aircraft-specific maintenance and parts manuals to members or sometimes even make them available for free on their websites. This is especially the case for aircraft that have been out of production for a long time.
- Reprinter companies—Reprinters such as Essco (www. esscoaircraft.com) and Pilot Mall (www.pilotmall.com/ category/aircraft-manuals) offer these documents for sale for many aircraft.

Service and parts manuals may be available in print or digital format, so you can choose based on your personal preference. Although there might be fees associated with obtaining these manuals, in the long run the expense is relatively minimal compared to the overall costs of aircraft operation. It's worth it to just get them.

The process for obtaining ADs may require some additional work. Original service manuals may not have all of them—or any of them—included. ADs are published by the FAA and can be found via FAA-provided website resources. But it will take some digging to do that on your own if a type club isn't providing you a customized list. Maintenance providers generally subscribe to services through which they enter an aircraft serial number and a list of components such as propellers or engines, and then they are provided with reports of applicable ADs for those items. For most owners, maintaining this subscription on their own is cost-prohibitive because they do not have enough aircraft or will not use it often enough to make it worth the price.

The good news is that if you have had maintenance done, your aircraft maintenance logs probably already include a list of applicable one-time or recurring ADs. In addition, the FAA makes all ADs publicly available on its website (see www.faa.gov/regulations_policies/airworthiness_directives/).

The list of ADs you have in your maintenance logs is likely just a list, not the full text of each AD. I encourage owners to go to the FAA website, find the corresponding ADs that are applicable to their aircraft and its components, and print them out. Build a binder of this printed material and keep it with the rest of the aircraft's maintenance logs. Then if you or a maintenance provider have any questions about the specifics of any ADs for your aircraft, the information will be readily available. If you want to go a little further, do the same thing for service bulletins. Although this will take some time, it isn't an ongoing commitment and it is worth having these documents available when maintenance is being conducted.

Having the applicable ADs, parts manuals, and service manuals is just part of being a good owner. It means that you will have all the available information needed to provide maintenance for your aircraft, determine what parts are appropriate if needed, and ensure you are complying with ADs. Take the time to collect and maintain these documents. It will also offer a good impression of your maintenance history if you ever go to sell the aircraft. You will look like a responsible owner who has worked hard to make sure the aircraft is in full compliance with all maintenance requirements.

Chapter 10

Organizing Your Aircraft's Logs for Better Maintenance

Not long ago, my wife and I purchased a 1947 Stinson 108-1 aircraft for pleasure flying. Compared to driving my truck, flying this aircraft also happens to be a much more enjoyable way for me to travel to give practical tests. A few months after we purchased the aircraft, we sent it to a mechanic friend of mine for the first annual inspection conducted under our ownership.

I wanted to have a good idea of what had been done on the aircraft and, to some degree, what was needed. Before the inspection, I spent time carefully going through the maintenance logs. In this case, the logbooks weren't too terribly messy; the aircraft's 17-year gap in flying before it was refurbished reduced the number of years of material that was entered. But I still uncovered some discrepancies.

Through a careful review, I found two airworthiness directives (ADs) that had been written off as not applicable, but a different mechanic later wrote them up as needing to be checked every 100 hours and 25 hours, respectively. The AD that had to be checked every 25 hours really inhibited the practical use of the aircraft! The good news was that after a bit of research, a discussion with my mechanic, and some updated logbook entries, we were able to show that the particular AD requiring a check every 25 hours was actually not applicable. The previous mechanic had just not understood that a replacement system installed that was different from the original meant that the AD did not apply to this specific aircraft.

The reason I tell this story before I share more detailed advice is that it illustrates the point that not every mechanic knows every aircraft inside and out. Owners have some level of responsibility for their own aircraft to ensure that when they provide logbooks and an aircraft to a maintenance professional for inspection or work, the records are in a condition such that the maintenance person can make sense of the logged history of the aircraft.

Many logbook sets for private aircraft are—to put it nicely—a mess. Handing over just a pile of books with no organization means that your mechanic will have to spend time sorting through what is there to get a better picture of the aircraft. This becomes even more difficult when it is the first time a mechanic has seen a particular aircraft make and model.

As an owner, a little work on your part ahead of time can make this less challenging. With that in mind, the rest of this chapter provides tips that can help you accomplish this.

Get Organized

The first major step is to get everything organized. The aircraft maintenance documents may include logbooks for engines, aircraft, and propellers; piles of major alteration forms (FAA Form 337); a stack of previous owners' registrations; maybe a few old airworthiness certificates; copies of maintenance invoices; promotional materials for the aircraft; supplemental type certificates (STCs) from various upgrades; and bills of sale—to name some of the specific, potentially relevant items. Mixed in with the more important documents, I have seen any number of other items ranging from pictures of the aircraft during refurbishment efforts to pilot logbooks of flights in the aircraft to a grandkid's drawing of the aircraft done one day at an airport.

Everything must be sorted into groups, including one pile that should be kept with the maintenance logs and another that perhaps will be kept in a separate box just as "aircraft history." Copies of previous airworthiness certificates, bills of sale, and registrations may be interesting to keep, but they do not need to be provided to the mechanic for review. These types of records can be kept separate from the current maintenance information, which is what is relevant to provide to the mechanic working on your aircraft.

If it helps, become familiar with your local office supply store. Binders with protective sleeves can be great to slide in and organize the often old, fragile copies of STC and Form 337 paperwork. If you want to get really crazy, put everything in order by the date the work was completed! I am only half joking here.

By sorting the wheat from the chaff, you essentially will minimize the pile that mechanics must go through when they evaluate and inspect your aircraft.

Create a List of Inspections and When They Are Due

Do you remember when you were getting your first pilot certificate and the examiner asked what inspections were required for the aircraft to be legally operated? As a pilot, it is your job to review the aircraft logs to make sure inspections have been done. As an aircraft owner, it's your job to make sure that the inspections are completed.

Do not try to keep track of all of the inspections in your head. I maintain a digital spreadsheet of the required inspections, and I also use it to track aircraft flight operation time. It helps me stay up to date on the schedule and timing for addressing all inspections and ADs so hopefully I will not let them pass.

The annual inspection is not the only thing you need to track. In addition, you need to track any pitot-static or transponder system checks, ELT inspections, VOR checks and GPS database requirements, and ADs.

There are many easy ways to track when inspections are due. For example, you can set reminders in your online calendar, create spreadsheets and update them as you use the aircraft, or use a low-tech method (which there is nothing wrong with), such as keeping a list in the aircraft or recording it on a whiteboard in the hangar. The point is, make sure you use some method to track when inspections must be completed. Don't just trust that the mechanic will give you a call when these inspection dates are approaching since he wants the business again this year.

Have ADs Tracked and Well Documented

I mentioned tracking ADs earlier in this chapter, but personal aircraft owners typically do not accomplish this task well. Many ADs on aircraft only need to be dealt with once, but some are "recurring," which means they must be addressed at regular time intervals. Compliance can be required either by specific dates or based on hours of use. The intervals of time between required compliance with recurring ADs can sometimes be relatively short, depending on the owner's use of the aircraft. This may occur more frequently than a yearly annual inspection.

On some aircraft, it is common to have 50-hour inspections on exhaust systems, 100-hour inspections on seat rails or (in the case of our Stinson) rudder cables, and 50-hour heater system inspections, to name only a few. In a good year of flying, an active pilot can easily miss these inspections between annuals and technically end up flying an aircraft that is not "airworthy" as a result.

Build a list of what ADs are applicable to your aircraft and keep a current record of the hours operated on the aircraft between annual inspections. This will help you avoid operating the aircraft beyond any required inspection times.

If you are not certain which ADs may apply to your aircraft, you can find all current ADs on the FAA website (www.faa.gov/regulations_policies/airworthiness_directives/). With a little digging based on the specific systems of your aircraft, you can get a better understanding of what ADs are required and why. In addition, you can sign up on the FAA's webpage to be notified by email of any new ADs that apply to your aircraft's make and model.

Insist on Detail in Mechanic's Documentation of Completed Work

I have too often seen logbook entries for an annual inspection simply state "annual completed" with no further detail. The mechanic completing the work should document if brakes were changed, if spark plugs were checked or changed, what type of oil or filter was used, etc. These little details will allow you as the owner, and any future maintenance providers, to have a clearer understanding of what exactly was done on an aircraft over time. This doesn't mean the mechanic needs to write a book explaining how many left turns it took on a screw to tighten down a bracket or seat clamp, but logging more detail about work as it is completed can help an owner document what items are commonly failing or may need attention on the aircraft.

This detail does not always have to be placed in the logbook entry for the aircraft; instead, it could refer to an invoice that includes more detail and that the owner keeps as a separate, deeper record of the aircraft's maintenance.

Know the Aircraft's History

It shouldn't be enough just to know that the last annual inspection was completed. It can be fun and informative to learn the deeper history of your aircraft. Much like your own pilot flight time logbook, the details in the maintenance logs only tell part of the story.

Going through the entire history of an aircraft can sometimes provide very interesting stories about its past. In the case of our Stinson, we found a 17-year gap without any maintenance work, and then an extensive two years of logbook entries, major alteration forms, and STC documentation. The aircraft had been parked for many years before a new owner endeavored to refurbish and upgrade the aircraft.

Going through the entire set of maintenance logs and any modification paperwork, an owner or maintenance professional will be able to determine what changes have been made to the aircraft, what new potential ADs may apply, or—if you are lucky—what ADs no longer need to be addressed at future inspections!

Go through the aircraft records, looking not only at engine, airframe, and propeller logs but also at any major alteration forms that may have been completed in order to fully understand what is installed on the aircraft.

After completing this review, do you have a concern that some of the records may be missing? This can certainly happen over the many years of an aircraft's life. The good news is that, if done properly, any major changes will be documented with the FAA, and the FAA is good about keeping records. For a small fee, the FAA will provide copies of aircraft records. You can find more information and submit a request on the FAA's "Aircraft Certification: Request Copies of Aircraft Records" webpage. (See the Reader Resources webpage at www.asa2fly.com/reader/avown for the direct link.)

I always encourage owners to do this for an aircraft they plan to keep for any length of time.

Make Copies and Store Them Safely

The final piece of advice I want to stress is to make copies of the aircraft logbooks and maintenance records and keep them in a place where they won't get destroyed.

Aircraft logbooks tell the history of an aircraft, but they also keep the aircraft legal to fly based on the documentation of work completed and required inspections. If these records go missing, get destroyed, or become no longer readable, the result is that the aircraft will no longer be able to be proven airworthy.

Many owners leave the logs in a hangar, in the aircraft, or with their mechanic without any protection for them. Hangars may get wet or burn, aircraft may get stolen or damaged, and mechanics can lose records or sometimes go out of business. I have seen each of these cases occur, resulting in missing or damaged aircraft logs and owners who are unable to document the maintenance history of their aircraft.

One of the first things I do with any aircraft I own—and which I strongly encourage all my customers to do—is to make copies. And I mean to make copies of everything.

Physical copies are a good start, but I typically use a scanner to also make digital copies. If you don't have a scanner, there are other options to digitize documents. Simply taking pictures of all of the pages using your phone is one easy way to do it. In addition, a wide variety of "scanner" apps that you can use on your phone or tablet device are available. Many of these turn the scans into PDF files.

This probably seems obvious, but make sure to keep the copies in a different place than the originals. This is one reason why I prefer scanned, digital copies. These can be saved using some form of online storage service—such as Dropbox, Google Drive, or Microsoft OneDrive—allowing the copies to survive any potential single computer failures. This may sound a little paranoid, but wouldn't you like to ensure that if your originals are damaged, you have a backup of the documents that will allow you to reconstruct the aircraft documentation history instead of having to re-do all the inspections?

. . .

I have personally found the recommendations I share in this chapter to be helpful not only for my own aircraft but also for other aircraft owners with whom I have worked. By maintaining detailed and organized logbooks as described here, you will make the mechanic's job easier, help ensure aircraft issues or requirements do not get missed, and occasionally even reduce the cost of inspections due to the fact that mechanics will need to spend less time on "the paperwork."

Chapter 11

Inoperative Equipment: What You Shouldn't Just Fly Without

"Oh, sorry, that hasn't worked for a while," the pilot said when he noticed I was trying to tune the DME in his aircraft while flying a couple of instrument approaches for his currency.

"What do you do when you fly an approach that requires DME?" I asked him, hoping the answer was that he didn't do those since it wasn't working.

"Well, I don't actually do many IFR approaches, but when I do run across that situation, I kind of rely on this," he said as he pointed to his yoke-mounted, portable GPS. This led to a longer discussion about why it was not appropriate to use non-certified equipment for instrument approaches. It also highlights a situation that I often see.

This is only one example of the many times I have discovered pilots flying aircraft with something broken that had obviously been inoperative for a significant period of time. These pilots had just "learned to live with it." Unfortunately, this approach causes them to either degrade their capabilities or to rely on equipment not properly certificated to get the job done.

It can be easy to let this happen. I'll admit that I have done it in aircraft I have owned. When something breaks, such as a panel light burning out, if we as owners don't find it critical to our typical flight, we may tend to ignore it or at least delay fixing it. In fact, many times as pilots we "learn to live without" certain things that don't work on our planes. However, doing this increases the risk encountered on every flight. These risks can range from conducting flights with less-than-ideal equipment resources to potential electrical fires or even failure of flight-critical systems.

Some of the most common equipment that pilots leave unfixed while operating their aircraft include second navigation and communication radios, DMEs, ADFs, panel lighting, and interior lights. But I have also seen aircraft flown with non-functional turn coordinators—and even flap motors and gear lights.

Certain things obviously pose greater risks than others when left inoperative, but anything left uncorrected poses a risk to the flight that should be mitigated. Inoperative equipment leaves pilots with fewer resources to complete their intended flight operations.

A non-functional DME can potentially leave a pilot forced to complete an instrument approach with non-certified equipment or without all the required information. An inoperative second glideslope indicator will leave the pilot without the backup for the primary glideslope indicator if it fails, which is the reason it was put in the aircraft in the first place. An inoperative light above a cylinder head temperature (CHT) gauge may leave the pilot unable to notice a developing problem if the temperatures are rising and it goes unnoticed on a night flight.

While leaving less-critical equipment such as a panel light inoperative may not seem like a big deal, such issues may indicate more serious problems. For example, the reason for the failure of a panel light could be a bulb or it could be an indication of a short somewhere in the system. If it is the latter, it could result in a bigger problem than just a faulty light—such as an electrical fire.

A potential side effect of just "learning to live with" items not working in an aircraft is that it develops complacency in pilots. This may lead to a tendency for them to fail to address more critical systems failures based on their developed habits of "getting it done" without all available equipment functioning.

What should pilots and owners do when there is inoperative equipment in their aircraft? I typically advise them to actively follow a "3-Rs" approach: Repair, Replace, or Remove.

Repair

If something is broken, talk with your maintenance provider and get it fixed. Fixing a broken piece of equipment ensures that any pilots flying the aircraft have all the proper resources available to them in the aircraft and reduces the risk that inoperative components could result in greater problems. I know there is a cost associated with repairing everything that is broken, but the cost of not fixing broken items could be more than money—it could become a matter of safety.

Replace

When something is broken, the best choice may not always be to simply try to fix it. Some equipment is difficult to fix, and it might be necessary to replace it instead. Most older equipment is getting harder to find direct replacements for, and if it breaks, this might present an opportunity to replace and upgrade at the same time. Is that old KX-170B radio not working in your instrument panel? Why not upgrade it to a modern GPS/Nav/Com unit that fits in the same position and that will upgrade the capabilities of your aircraft?

Remove

In some cases, certain items that are inoperative can simply be removed. Most pilots are not flying NDB approaches anymore, especially if their aircraft are equipped with IFR-capable GPS. If your aircraft has a non-functional ADF in it, have it removed at your next annual; this will eliminate the potential that other problems will be generated by the inoperative device or from whatever is causing it to not work properly. Some equipment will never work again. If you still have a LORAN in your aircraft, it will never get a signal no matter what your avionics shop does to it since the LORAN towers have long been turned off.

Removing inoperative, unused, and unnecessary equipment will mitigate any potential risk they present, clean up your plane, and also reduce the overall empty weight of the aircraft in many cases and offer more usable payload. If you have equipment that is really not being used and is not required, consider removing it altogether from the aircraft as a viable option.

. . .

You may wonder, what's the worst thing I have seen "let go"? I have a wide variety of examples, but one I vividly remember is showing up to a checkride only to find that the pilot had taped down the breaker for his aircraft's alternator. When I queried why the alternator breaker was taped down, he answered, "It keeps popping, the tape keeps it from doing that." I followed this answer with a discussion of the risks that were present with a breaker that was popping and what could go wrong if it was forcibly held in place and not allowed to do its intended job. Obviously, we didn't complete the checkride until the problem was fixed.

The main point is that it is easy for owners to get "comfortable" with some inoperative equipment in their aircraft. However, doing this may cause them to take additional risks and may precipitate other problems during flight operations. Flying with inoperative equipment is a risk that pilots should not allow to become a regular part of their routine. As an owner, you can mitigate the risks of inoperative equipment by actively dealing with current problems to avoid developing future ones.

I will go into more detail about inoperative equipment in Chapter 14, which covers minimum equipment lists (MELs), kinds of operation lists (KOLs), and the regulations that apply when determining whether you can fly with certain inoperable equipment.

Chapter 12

Completing Your Own Maintenance: What Can You—and What Should You—Do Yourself?

If you are not an FAA-certificated maintenance professional, you're not allowed to change the engine on your own aircraft like you can if you are a mechanically inclined individual who works on classic cars. However, this does not mean that you can't do any work on your aircraft. In fact, aircraft owners are allowed to do quite a few things that are part of the day-to-day maintenance of an aircraft.

Completing some of this work on your own will not only save you money but it will also give you a more thorough understanding of your aircraft and make you more likely to catch potential problems on a preflight inspection. It can also make annual maintenance completed by your mechanic go a little quicker or smoother.

What are all the specific maintenance tasks you are allowed to complete? A detailed list of what you can do as an FAA-certificated pilot and/or owner of an aircraft can be found in 14 CFR Part 43, Appendix A (c). This lists specific work that is considered "preventative maintenance."

With this in mind, the question then becomes, what maintenance "should" you complete yourself? It can be helpful to know what someone with experience in the industry and who has owned aircraft recommends the average owner do on their own.

The answer depends a little bit on the owner's background and his or her mechanical aptitude. Not everyone is mechanically inclined, at least at the outset. I would say that even if that is the case for you, if you have been smart and dedicated enough to become a pilot, then there definitely are things you could be taught to manage on your own aircraft.

Most pilots are comfortable adding oil, fueling the aircraft, adding air to a tire if it is low, or perhaps even filling a hydraulic fluid reservoir for brakes. But what about work that goes beyond this? There are a few maintenance tasks that I encourage owners to learn to complete.

As a first step, I often encourage owners to learn how to change bulbs for navigation, landing, beacon, and strobe lights. These are pretty easy to change on most aircraft, and having that capability can make the difference that allows you to spend 10 quick minutes changing them yourself to get off on a planned night flight rather than having to delay your flight for a day until a maintenance provider can change the bulbs. In some aircraft, landing lights can be a little more complicated, especially when a cowling needs to be removed. On many aircraft, this can best be accomplished with the assistance of a second person; even just a friend who can help hold things in place may be enough.

Changing the oil can also be a great thing to be able to do on your own aircraft. Instead of having to bring the aircraft to your maintenance shop in between annuals—every 50 or even every 25 hours, depending on how often you change the oil—you can complete this in your hangar typically in less than an hour. The complexity of changing the oil can vary based on the aircraft, but in many cases, draining the oil is very simple. Many aircraft are equipped with quick drains (and if yours is not, it can be very affordable to install one). These allow the oil to easily be drained via a funnel to a collector bucket, in some cases without even requiring removal of the cowlings.

Changing your own oil is not always the cleanest job, but it doesn't have to be terribly messy either. If you aren't comfortable doing it yourself, get someone to teach you. Draining the oil is not that hard. A little planning ahead with a good funnel, perhaps a hose, and a collection bag can make that part relatively mess-free.

Changing the oil filter can be a little messier, but it can really help to use a strategically placed plastic bag for the filter to fall into as you unscrew it. Make sure you know how to properly safety wire the filter back in place when you install the new one. And I'll share a tip based on experience: make sure you have drained the oil before taking the filter off. If you don't, you will be draining much of the oil via the filter, which makes a much bigger mess.

It can also be a good idea to learn to change a spark plug. Properly removing a spark plug and gapping and installing a new one is a project that is easily accessible and that can keep a pilot flying in the event of a badly fouled or cracked plug. Changing a spark plug does require more tools than some other maintenance work, and you must be able to determine which plug is affected, unless you want to change them all. At a minimum, I encourage owners to have a few extra plugs (or even a full set) available for their aircraft in case they are needed. The local maintenance provider may be able to change a plug, but they probably will not always have the one you need in stock. If you always have extra plugs, that problem can be avoided.

I certainly recommend that owners know how to charge, and potentially even change, a battery in their aircraft. I will certainly admit to leaving a master switch on more than once in my life, and the ability to charge my own battery in my hangar allowed me to get my aircraft back up and running again. Different aircraft have their batteries located in different places, so take the time to learn where your battery is located, if accessing it requires any access panels to be removed, and how to charge the battery if it is inadvertently drained.

You can also change your aircraft's battery on your own, if you find it necessary to do so. Obviously, batteries don't always fail right at the time of an annual inspection. If you find your aircraft's battery just isn't holding a charge and providing the starting power you need, it is something that in many aircraft you can easily change between annuals.

I also encourage owners to learn how to properly remove seats in their airplanes. In many mid-sized aircraft, especially those with six or more seats, removing some seats can provide the owner with a greater ability to pack in gear, collapsible bicycles, or any other piles of stuff more easily. Even in certain four-seat aircraft, removing the back seats can be a quick and easy way to make room to put gear for a longer trip or simply to haul some bulky equipment. It's important to note that whenever you do this, you should make sure that the floor of the aircraft is rated for the weight you will be putting on it. Also be aware that in many cases, you will be required to have an "alternate" weight and balance for different seat configurations properly documented by an FAA certificated maintenance provider.

I have had multiple weight and balance documents prepared for many of the aircraft I have owned or operated to allow for additional weight-carrying capacity (when weight is reduced by removing seats) and sometimes more importantly to provide additional room in the cabin for either passengers or gear. There is nothing that prohibits you from having several weight and balance documents for the same aircraft in different configurations. This allows you to use the one that represents how the aircraft is configured at the time you are operating it.

In many aircraft, the reality is that a full complement of passengers cannot be carried when the aircraft has a full fuel load, anyway, so removing a seat or two may allow passengers to more easily enter, exit, or move around in the cabin area, especially if the seat by the door is removed.

If your aircraft will be equipped with skis for part of the year, you may find it is worth learning how to put skis on and off the aircraft. This can be completed by an owner if no weight and balance changes are needed.

A related task is changing a tire, which is also possible for owners to do on their own aircraft. While many owners draw the line short of this task, you might want to learn how to change an aircraft tire in case it's ever necessary. If you plan to do this, it also might be worth investing in a set of jacks for your aircraft to help you complete this process. When changing an aircraft tire, the aircraft isn't typically jacked up using an average floor jack. Lifting an aircraft without using the proper jacking points can potentially cause damage.

With these allowed, owner-completed maintenance procedures in mind, following is a basic list of items that I think every aircraft owner should consider having in their hanger, beyond the basic tools that most individuals likely already have.

- **A battery charger.** Make sure it is the right voltage; many aircraft cannot use the typical commercially available 12-volt chargers and require a higher voltage.
- **Safety wire and safety wire pliers.** These may look confusing at first, but a brief tutorial from a knowledgeable mechanic or friend can quickly teach you the tricks. Many items on aircraft require safety wire to secure them in place.
- **An oil filter wrench.** If you will be doing your own oil changes, a good oil filter wrench will save you lots of headaches. Even though filters may be only finger-tightened to start, they always seem to be overtight and suddenly won't budge when it comes time to remove them.
- **Spark plug socket.** Available in different sizes, this tool is basically a deep socket that fits the spark plugs on an aircraft. Many of them have a rubber grommet to help hold the spark plug in the socket. If you will be changing your own spark plugs, this tool can make your life easier. Although it's not as important for the process of taking the plug out, using a socket when installing a plug can make it easier to hold it in place and can allow you to finger-tighten the plug without it flopping around or dropping.
- **Aircraft jacks.** These can be kind of expensive and may be hard to find for certain aircraft. While maintenance shops will usually have lightweight jacks for most common aircraft, if you have a heavier or unique aircraft, you may need larger jacks or ones that have specialty attachment points. In that case, it can be worth investing in jacks for your specific aircraft, not only if you want to do your own tire changes but also because

having the proper equipment available for your maintenance provider can make it easier for them to complete your annual inspections.

These are just a few of the items you might want to consider. Certainly, there are any number of additional tools you could have—and maybe can convince yourself you need—for your aircraft or hangar. With the equipment I have seen collected in some hangars, the owners could probably build an aircraft as well as a factory!

The FAA Safety Team (FAASTeam) offers a publication titled "Maintenance Aspects of Owning Your Own Aircraft," which I encourage owners to review. (See the Reader Resources webpage at www.asa2fly.com/reader/avown.) This publication offers recommendations of other items that owners can regularly monitor or service to keep their aircraft flying in the best possible condition between visits to an FAA-certificated mechanic for regularly scheduled inspections or other work. This document also includes a series of checklists an owner or pilot might choose to follow to more thoroughly inspect an aircraft between annual inspections. Each checklist does not need to be completed on every flight, but by working the checklists into a regular pattern of owner inspection, it can help a pilot or owner identify areas of concern that may indicate a trend toward failure and catch problems before they become catastrophic or just more expensive to address.

Chapter 13

Items You Should Own and Keep in Your Aircraft

Aircraft owners usually have standard items they carry on their aircraft, such as charts, a handheld radio, batteries for a headset, oil, rags, emergency gear (depending on the terrain over which they will fly), a multi-function tool (that at a minimum contains pliers, both Phillips and flat-head screwdrivers, and a wire cutter), a tire pressure gauge, some safety wire, and the obvious, duct tape.

In addition, below are a few less-common items that I believe should be on every airplane. Carrying these items might allow you to get home when you might otherwise be stranded.

Less Common Items to Keep on Your Airplane

Extra Light Bulbs

14 CFR Part 43 Appendix A, part (c), provides a specific list of "preventative maintenance" work that pilots can do on their aircraft. This includes changing bulbs. In many general aviation aircraft, replacing bulbs is a pretty simple task. But many airports will not have these items in stock, and if it's 9:00 p.m. and dark when you are trying to get back home with a burnt-out landing or navigation light, it could prevent you from being able to complete your flight in accordance with regulations. Having an extra landing light, an extra beacon bulb, and spare bulbs for your navigation lights (and knowing how to change them) can allow you to replace them quickly and keep flying.

While no one might notice a burnt-out light bulb when you are leaving from a non-towered rural airport, if you are operating from busier or towered airports, it is more likely that someone will notice. Operational lights are obviously important for safety while in flight so that other aircraft can properly identify your direction of flight. But having extra bulbs on hand will also keep you legal and help avoid a situation where you are tempted to "just fly home" with a burnt-out light to get it fixed. Once on a return trip from Meigs Field, my fellow pilot and I noticed that our aircraft's left navigation light had burned out and we made what I now look back on as a poor decision to go anyway, hoping that the Tower didn't notice or say anything.

Extra Spark Plugs

Have you ever fouled out a spark plug or had one crack? Keeping just one extra set of plugs in your airplane doesn't take up much space and can be a simple solution to this potential maintenance problem. Per 14 CFR Part 43, you are not supposed to change spark plugs on your own (this should be done by an A&P or IA certificated mechanic). However, it is more likely that you can find a mechanic at an airport to do this work if you have the parts than it is that the local FBO will happen to have the plugs specific to your aircraft in stock.

Extra Fuel Cap

A loose fuel cap can easily fall off during a taxi, run-up, or takeoff. (I know you would never forget to tighten the fuel cap after refueling, but a line guy might, right?) Obviously, an aircraft cannot be flown without a fuel cap (for reasons such as spillage and fuel flow, to name a few), so if you happen to lose a fuel cap, you could be stuck for days waiting for a replacement to arrive. Having an extra fuel cap on hand for your aircraft provides a simple fix to a problem that could leave you stranded. Purchasing an extra fuel cap is not terribly expensive, and it will even fit in the aircraft's glove compartment. If you lose a fuel cap and your luck is anything like mine, there is very little chance, even after long and thorough searches of the ramp, taxiway, runway, and all the weeds around the airport, that you will find the lost fuel cap. That extra one you packed will get you home.

Cowling Screws

For most aircraft, there is a minimum number of cowling screws that must be in place for the aircraft to be flown. Vibration and rattles sometimes shake a few loose. For this reason, it's a great idea to include several extra screws in your "save a flight" kit; they can easily be installed with a multi-tool screwdriver on a preflight. It's safer to replace missing screws when you notice them than to fly with less than the desired full number.

Jump Plug Adapter or Power Pack

I have seen cases in which a dead battery, without any way to provide external power to "jump" it, absolutely killed a flight. A battery can quickly be drained by something as simple as a passenger leaving an entry door light on or the pilot forgetting to shut off a master switch.

For aircraft that do not allow traditional jumper cables to be attached to provide external power, special plug adapters are often available that fit into the side of the aircraft. You can usually find these for sale at any aviation supplier for less than $100. These plug adapters stick into the special power port on the side of the plane, allowing you to attach traditional jumper cables to that plug and jump-start your aircraft. If your aircraft has a 12-volt system, this could even allow it to be jump-started from a car.

There are also great rechargeable power packs (and some very compact USB rechargeable ones) that you could take along to allow you to be self-sufficient if you will be at airports with limited services. Make sure you follow the proper external power starting procedures as described by your aircraft manufacturer (this is typically explained in the POH). Having the proper connectors to attach external power can get you home when you otherwise would be forced to seek a hotel.

I once flew to an island airport with a friend to take his friends to a special anniversary dinner. On the flight over, we didn't notice that a passenger left the over-door cabin light on, and that light does not shut off when the master switch is off. While we waited for them to finish their dinner, the battery slowly drained, leaving us unable to start the airplane.

The airport on that island does not have an FBO. There are no cars to use for a jump-start since no vehicles are allowed on the island, and a horse is of no use in jump-starting an aircraft! And it was also late in the season when most services on the island are closed. However, we quickly plugged in the Piper Plug and Jump adapter, attached a small portable rechargeable jump pack, and started the airplane. Without these two tools, we would have been stuck!

· · ·

Each of these items are things that many aircraft owners do not normally carry with them. They are all small and require a relatively minimal cost to acquire. While they aren't all tools or parts that pilots personally directly use themselves, a mechanic may need these items to fix your airplane (as in the case of spark plugs, for example). 14 CFR Part 43, Appendix A, Section (c), gives a list of preventative maintenance tasks that pilots can complete on their own—assuming they are capable of doing so. However, if you do not have the needed items to complete the work and the FBO doesn't stock them, what could be a minor fix may turn into a major delay and inconvenience.

If you compare the cost of purchasing these items with what you'll pay if you don't have them when you need them (the costs of a hotel, shipping, service, and other expenses you could have avoided), it is a small price to pay and well worth it to acquire these items and add them to the baggage compartment of your plane.

In addition, a few basic tools will help make each of the above things potentially more useful. Below are the tools I make sure are in a kit of every aircraft I own or operate.

Basic Tools Every Pilot Should Carry

The tools listed here are some of the less common ones pilots might consider, but I encourage every pilot (even renters) to carry the following basic tools in their aircraft at all times. (Some of these can be combined by carrying a good multi-tool such as a Leatherman.)

- Phillips screwdriver (with multiple-sized tips)
- Flat-head screwdriver
- Needle-nose pliers
- Adjustable crescent wrench
- Basic socket and wrench set
- Safety wire and safety wire pliers
- A few cable ties
- Duct tape

Chapter 14

Deciding If You Can Fly with Inoperative Equipment: MELs, KOLs, and Beyond

"Can I fly my aircraft if the _____ isn't working?"

It's a common question I get from aircraft owners with whom I work.

"How about if I fly the aircraft just to get it home to my mechanic to fix it?"

These questions sound simple, but they can easily end up driving owners deep into confusion about minimum equipment lists (MELs), master MELs, kinds of operation lists (KOLs), and more when trying to discern the applicability of allowable inoperative equipment for different types of operations under 14 CFR §91.205.

Many owners get confused about the applicability of 14 CFR §91.205. This really is about what equipment the aircraft must have installed for the pilot to be allowed to conduct the type of operations (VFR or IFR). If the equipment is listed in §91.205, it must be in working condition during applicable operations. If one of the items listed in that regulation isn't working, no MEL, MMEL, or KOL will allow you to fly without it operating.

Assuming those basic instruments are still functional, if anything else is not working, it is up to the pilot to determine if the aircraft has an MEL (this would be an FAA-approved document specific to the aircraft tail number), if there is a master minimum equipment list (MMEL) that the manufacturer publishes, or if there is a kinds of operation list (KOL) that applies to the make and model of aircraft.

Most light, personally flown, general aviation aircraft have not had MELs established for them. But MELs might be available for aircraft that were previously operated on a charter certificate or, in some cases, for larger aircraft.

MMELs are not available for every aircraft, but a few common general aviation (GA) aircraft do have them. The Piper Seminole is a great example (Figure 10).

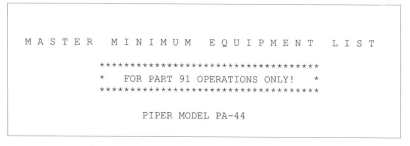

```
M A S T E R   M I N I M U M   E Q U I P M E N T   L I S T

        * * * * * * * * * * * * * * * * * * * * * * * * * * * * * * * * * *
        *    FOR PART 91 OPERATIONS ONLY!    *
        * * * * * * * * * * * * * * * * * * * * * * * * * * * * * * * * * *

                    PIPER MODEL PA-44
```

Figure 10. The Piper PA-44 Seminole is one of the common GA aircraft for which MMELs are available.

On the FAA's webpage "Master Minimum Equipment List (MMEL) by Manufacturer," you will find drop-down lists of the aircraft makes and models that have MMELs published and listed with the FAA. (See the Reader Resources at www.asa2fly.com/reader/avown.) If your aircraft can be found here, it may be a good idea to have a copy of your MMEL in case you ever need to evaluate if you can fly with something not working on your aircraft. Keep in mind that a MMEL or MEL must be approved for use by the FAA for the specific tail number or its operation for it to be applicable, but the skill of how to use these documents is often lacking.

Kinds of operation lists (KOLs) are a more recent invention and are increasingly being found in POHs for modern aircraft. Whichever one the aircraft has (MEL, MMEL, or KOL) is what you will use to determine if you can fly when something isn't working. Think of it as a "permission list."

MELs, MMELs, and KOLs do not tell a pilot what must be working; they tell the pilot what is allowed to be "not working." If it isn't listed in the document, was originally installed, or is a part of the type certificate for the aircraft, it has to be working. To fly without something exempted on one of these lists requires involvement of a maintenance professional, probably disabling the piece of equipment, some placarding, and potentially a special flight permit.

It really is that simple. These lists are permission lists that help you determine if you can fly when something isn't working or if you need to get help from maintenance!

One example I often use in practical tests is the MMEL on the Piper Seminole. While 14 CFR §91.205 indicates that an aircraft must have a generator or alternator, the Seminole has two (alternators). So I ask the applicant whether we could fly if one wasn't working when we ran the aircraft up for a preflight. Applicants often struggle through the MMEL (if they even know how to find it) and discover that the document is silent on the topic of alternators. If an item is not listed on the MMEL as allowed to be inoperative (or in this case, one of the two installed alternators allowed to be inoperative), it means that the item must be functional.

Another example on the same aircraft is the cockpit shoulder harnesses. The MMEL lists that two are installed and that the right-side harness may be inoperative as long as that seat remains unoccupied (Figure 11). Although this sounds simple, it really does end up a major confusion point on many practical tests.

```
---------------------------------------------------------------------------
| U.S. DEPARTMENT OF TRANSPORTATION                                         |
|                                                                           |
|                                           MASTER MINIMUM EQUIPMENT LIST   |
| FEDERAL AVIATION ADMINISTRATION                                           |
|-------------------------------------------------------------------------- |
| AIRCRAFT:                        | REVISION NO: 6          | PAGE:        |
|                                  |                         |              |
|           PIPER MODEL PA-44      | DATE: 01/23/2003        | 25-1         |
|-------------------------------------------------------------------------- |
|                         1. | 2. NUMBER INSTALLED                          |
| SYSTEM &                   |------------------------------------------    |
| SEQUENCE        ITEM       |  3. NUMBER REQUIRED FOR DISPATCH             |
| NUMBERS                    |  ------------------------------------------  |
|--------------------------- |     | 4. REMARKS OR EXCEPTIONS               |
| 25  EQUIPMENT/FURNISHINGS  |     |                                        |
|                                                                           |
| 1.  Cockpit Shoulder   B | 2 | 1 | Right side may be inoperative          |
|     Harness                       | provided seat remains unoccupied.     |
|                                                                           |
| 2.  Passenger Seat     C | - | 0 | May be inoperative provided:           |
|                                   | a) Seat does not block an             |
|                                   |    emergency exit, and                |
|                                   | b) Affected seats are blocked         |
|                                   |    and placarded "DO NOT              |
|                                   |    OCCUPY".                           |
|                                   |                                       |
|                                   | NOTE:  A seat with an inoperative     |
|                                   |        seatbelt is considered         |
|                                   |        inoperative.                   |
---------------------------------------------------------------------------
```

Figure 11. *For example only; do not use for flight planning.* MMEL for the Piper PA-44, showing that the right-side cockpit shoulder harness (one of the two that are installed) may be inoperative if that seat remains unoccupied.

Again referring to the MMEL for the PA-44, we can see that a heater system would be allowed to be inoperative (assuming it had been evaluated by a maintenance professional, disabled, and placarded as inoperative) and the aircraft could still conduct flights (Figure 12). Flying without an operational heater would obviously be a little chilly in winter climates, but in someplace warm such as Florida, it may not be an issue that the owner decides to immediately address with a fix or replacement.

U.S. DEPARTMENT OF TRANSPORTATION

FEDERAL AVIATION ADMINISTRATION

MASTER MINIMUM EQUIPMENT LIST

AIRCRAFT: PIPER MODEL PA-44	REVISION NO: 6 DATE: 01/23/2003	PAGE: 21-1

SYSTEM & SEQUENCE NUMBERS / ITEM	1.	2. NUMBER INSTALLED	3. NUMBER REQUIRED FOR DISPATCH	4. REMARKS OR EXCEPTIONS
21 AIR CONDITIONING				
1. Heater	C	1	0	(M)
2. Air Conditioner System	C	1	0	(M)
3. Fresh Air Fan	C	1	0	
4. Heater Hour Meter	C	1	0	(O)

Figure 12. *For example only; do not use for flight planning.* MMEL for the PA-44 showing heater requirements.

The examples above using a MMEL for the PA-44 work exactly the same as if the aircraft had an approved MEL for the specific aircraft. The only difference is that a MEL is specific to an individual tail numbered aircraft and lists the specific components installed that may be beyond the minimum factory equipment, while the MMEL instead applies to the broader aircraft model (within a make of aircraft by a manufacturer).

In another example, the Cirrus SR20 has a KOL and directs pilots differently depending on if they will be operating at some points in IFR or VFR conditions. For example, the KOL allows a pilot to operate with only Alternator or Battery 1 operational in VFR flight, but requires that both Alternators and Batteries 1 and 2 be operational if the pilot will be operating in IFR conditions (Figure 13).

Kinds of Operation

The SR20 is equipped and approved for the following type operations:

- VFR day and night.
- IFR day and night.

Serials 1337 and subsequent with SRV configuration: The airplane is equipped and approved for the following type operations:

- VFR day and night.

Kinds of Operation Equipment List

The following listing summarizes the equipment required under Federal Aviation Regulations (FAR) Part 23 for airworthiness under the listed kind of operation. Those minimum items of equipment necessary under the operating rules are defined in FAR Part 91 and FAR Part 135 as applicable.

· Note ·

All references to types of flight operations on the operating limitations placards are based upon equipment installed at the time of Airworthiness Certificate issuance.

System, Instrument, and/or Equipment	Kinds of Operation				Remarks, Notes, and/or Exceptions
	VFR Day	VFR Nt.	IFR Day	IFR Nt.	
Communications					
Electrical Power					
Battery 1	1	1	1	1	
Battery 2	—	—	1	1	
Alternator 1	1	1	1	1	
Alternator 2	—	—	1	1	erials 1337 & subs / SRV standard onfiguration: ALT 2 not applicable.

Figure 13. *For example only; do not use for flight planning.* Kinds of operation list (KOL) for Cirrus SR20.

With all this in mind, there's no reason to be confused about these documents anymore: Think of them as permission slips. If the document allows the pilot to operate with something inoperative, it will say so. If the pilot doesn't have one of these documents, or available documents are mute on a component or system, then a pilot should consider that component or system as required to be working in order to fly.

So, back to the original question at the beginning of this chapter: Can an owner fly if something on the aircraft is not working?

Unless there is a MEL, MMEL,[1] or KOL that specifically lists something that can be inoperative while still allowing the flight to be completed, you probably cannot legally operate the aircraft. Certainly, you will not be able to operate the aircraft without the help of a maintenance professional who can determine if the type certificate for the aircraft requires the component and, if not, can properly document and disable that piece of equipment.

How far does this go? Does it mean that I can't fly my aircraft if it has a broken dome light? Technically, that is probably true. I know that things like this go unfixed on a regular basis. But a line must be drawn somewhere, and the FAA wants that line to be drawn by a maintenance professional, not by pilots who think they can "just get the flight done" without that left flap that fell off the aircraft on the last landing.

1. You can see if there is an FAA-approved, manufacturer-provided MMEL for your aircraft at http://fsims.faa.gov/PICResults.aspx?mode=Publication&doctype=MMEL.

Chapter 15

The Special Flight Permit

Now that we have talked about what you can and cannot fly with inoperative, it's probably important that we talk about what you can do if you find something inoperative and need to get the aircraft to where maintenance can be completed (assuming it is not at an airport where that is possible or desired).

According to the FAA, a special flight permit, commonly referred to as a "ferry permit",[2]

> may be issued for an aircraft that may not currently meet applicable airworthiness requirements, but is capable of safe flight, for the following purposes:
>
> - Flying aircraft to a point for repairs, alterations, maintenance, or storage (for example, ferrying an aircraft from point A to point B).
> - Delivering new aircraft to the base of a purchaser or to a storage point.
> - Conducting production flight tests.
> - Evacuating an aircraft from impending danger.
> - Conducting customer demonstration flights in new production aircraft that have passed or completed production flight tests.
> - Excess weight operations.

---

2. "Special Airworthiness Certificate: Special Flight Permit," United States Department of Transportation, Federal Aviation Administration (website), last modified September 4, 2013, https://www.faa.gov/aircraft/air_cert/airworthiness_certification/sp_awcert/sp_flt_permit/.

The FAA also notes:

> The special flight permit does not authorize flight over a country other than the United States without permission of that country.

In most cases, owners use a special flight permit to get an aircraft to a maintenance provider (or to the maintenance provider of their choice) when a component has failed that does not adversely affect the ability of the aircraft to be safely operated. Some examples include if an aircraft's auxiliary fuel pump has failed, an instrument avionics component isn't working, or the flap motors have failed and the aircraft cannot deploy the flaps for landing. The reasons for getting a ferry permit can vary wildly. It is even possible that a special flight permit may be issued for a twin-engine aircraft to be operated with one engine inoperative. Imagine that takeoff!

Probably the most common reason for owners to need special flight permits issued is if they miss the deadline for an annual inspection. This has been the case with many aircraft I have been involved with when the owners were unable to get the aircraft from their home airport to the maintenance provider due to weather delays.

No matter the reason, if a special flight permit is required, the aircraft's owner or operator will have to contact the local FAA office, provide details on a form, and have a maintenance professional evaluate the reason that such a permit is needed. Assuming the maintenance professional (typically an A&P or an Inspection Authorization FAA-certificated mechanic) then determines that the aircraft can be safely operated for the intended flight, the inspector must sign the FAA special flight permit form and make a notation in the aircraft's records. In some cases, an FAA maintenance representative may also elect to inspect the aircraft prior to issuance of the special flight permit.

The required forms include a completed FAA Form 8130-6, Application for U.S. Airworthiness Certificate, on which the applicant can indicate the reason for seeking a special flight permit under section II, option 8, of the form. When the FAA receives this, it will issue an approval form back to the requestor, and that form must then be signed by the involved maintenance professional before any flights may be conducted.

It is worth noting that the permit issued by the FAA office will likely have some limitations. Most special flight permits must be completed in VFR, daytime conditions and do not allow for anyone to be in the aircraft other than required crewmembers. That means you would not be allowed to take passengers, your flight instructor, or technically even your dog. An operation under a special flight permit is not a pleasure flight; its purpose is to allow you to get your aircraft to the place where the needed maintenance can be completed (or to move it for another approved purpose indicated on FAA Form 8130-6).

More information about the FAA Special Airworthiness Certificate—Special Flight Permit program can be found in the Airworthiness Certification section of the FAA's website. (Direct links are listed on the Reader Resources webpage at www.asa2fly.com/reader/avown.)

Chapter 16

Modifying Your Aircraft to Enhance Performance

Your aircraft is not like a Jeep that you purchase and then can add parts onto from the local auto parts store to upgrade, modify, or tweak it. However, this does not mean that your aircraft cannot be changed from how it was originally delivered by the manufacturer. Many pilots modify their aircraft with bigger engines, bigger tires, floats, skis, vortex generators, more fuel tanks, different propellers, or any number of other performance-enhancing modifications.

The most common modifications typically made by owners include bigger engines, performance enhancements to improve short-field takeoffs, or fuel tanks to expand range. When considering whether to make changes like this on an aircraft, I highly recommend taking some time and doing your homework before starting the process. When considering a specific modification, I encourage owners to build a budget sheet that includes all the items that will be required to complete it. If you want to add a bigger engine, you may encounter costs beyond just the cost of the engine itself. There will of course be some labor costs, but it may also require a new engine mount, modification of the engine mount, paying for the supplemental type certificate (STC) approval for the modification, changing fuel lines, perhaps a different propeller, or even installation of different engine or fuel monitoring gauges according to approved installation processes for some engine modifications. These ancillary costs can quickly take an engine upgrade from the cost of only the engine to well over double that amount to complete the entire modification. It is worth knowing this ahead of time before you have your favorite mechanic start taking your aircraft apart.

With that warning in mind, let's look at some of the most common modifications that owners consider making on their aircraft.

Engines

More power is always a good thing, right? Well, maybe.

Many owners look to increase engine size when they consider modifying their aircraft or are doing engine overhauls. In some cases, this can be accomplished with an easy swap and a quick approval of a different engine on the same airframe. In other cases, it can require costly modification of mounts, may require different fuel lines (of larger capacity to feed engines that require more fuel), and sometimes can come with expensive "STC fees" to pay the owner of an STC for the right to use the approval for a particular install.

It's worth checking into these things before you go forward. If you haven't found any major hiccups after evaluating the requirements, you may decide that this modification is worth making, as more power can result in some improvements.

A bigger engine often will increase the approved gross weight at which an aircraft can be operated. It will not always result in a huge increase in payload because the new engine will probably weigh more than the previous, smaller-horsepower engine, but an incremental increase in payload is typical. Performance will also often improve in aircraft modified with larger engines, commonly including improvements in climb rate, maximum altitude, cruise speed (to some degree), and short-field takeoff distance.

Although there are benefits of bigger engines, they also come with some drawbacks. A bigger engine on the front of an aircraft often moves the center of gravity (CG) forward. In some cases, a forward shift in CG can make it difficult to stay within the CG envelope with only front seat passengers, and this may require the pilot to operate with some ballast in the rear of the aircraft. Along with CG changes, bigger engines burn more fuel. Without a corresponding increase in the aircraft's fuel capacity, its range may be decreased even with a slight increase in cruising speed that is gained.

When it comes to the speed increases gained from bigger engines, there is always a level of diminishing return on investment. Bigger engines typically provide more of a benefit in weight-hauling capacity than they do in speed gained. Additionally, airframes have operating limitations for speed that are not typically allowed to be increased just because a bigger engine is installed. If an aircraft has a 180-horsepower engine but has a maximum operating speed of 140 knots and typically cruises at 120 knots, installing a 400-horsepower engine may make it possible to pull the aircraft through the air at speeds greater than 140 knots. However, if the limitation on the airframe has not been increased, it would be an imprudent pilot who operated this aircraft above the speed limitation.

The engine itself is not the only modification that will enhance horsepower. Specialized exhaust systems can also provide some increase in performance on aircraft for which they are available. Sometimes considered "the poor man's engine upgrade," these exhaust systems can provide a few extra horsepower and a little extra "oomph" on aircraft that need a little climb help. It is amazing how much help the extra 15 horsepower can be on a 140-horsepower Cherokee with an exhaust system that makes it perform more like 155 horsepower. That is an increase in horsepower of approximately 10 percent on the same engine.

For most aircraft, there will be an engine that seems to be the best "fit for the airframe." If there are multiple possible upgrade options for your airplane, talk with other owners of the same aircraft make and model who have completed engine upgrades. In some cases, it becomes a thrust-to-weight ratio balancing act. You may be surprised: Bigger may be better in some cases, but the "biggest" may not always be the best.

Propellers

An easy and not terribly expensive change many pilots choose to make, especially on fixed-pitch propeller aircraft, is changing props to get a different "pitch" for better cruise or climb performance. On an airframe and engine, props may be approved that are of different lengths or pitch to accomplish better climb rates or cruise performance, respectively.

When considering different fixed-pitch propellers, it's important to understand that a propeller with a pitch set for climb performance is giving up cruise performance. It will get you out of a shorter field in less runway and will climb to an altitude quicker, but when it gets there, it will be slower in cruise. A propeller set for a cruise pitch will take more runway and climb distance, but once it is there it will cruise more quickly. With that said, my own personal experience has been that climb pitch propellers tend to provide more benefit in terms of their climb performance than cruise pitch propellers do in overall gained speed. But that can vary to some degree based on the airframe. When you are looking at changing a fixed-pitch propeller, talk with a good propeller shop that knows your make and model of aircraft and its engine to realistically discuss the possible benefits and what you are trying to accomplish.

If your aircraft has a constant speed propeller or you are considering changing it to one, some additional modifications are possible.

Changing an aircraft's fixed-pitch propeller over to a constant-speed propeller will effectively allow the pilot to have the benefits of both a climb and cruise performance propeller in the same aircraft. This is essentially the main benefit of a constant-speed propeller. Adding a constant-speed propeller system to an aircraft historically equipped with a fixed-pitch propeller will typically require an STC to be completed and will add some weight and maintenance cost to the aircraft footprint. Is it worth it? Well, it depends on what you want to do with the aircraft. I have a friend who modifies Cessna 170 aircraft from their original 145-horsepower, fixed-pitch-propeller equipped engines to constant-speed propeller systems on 210-horsepower engines, and they perform like beasts. Most of them are sold off to operators in the bush in Alaska and northern Canada. Is it worth it for them? Yup. However, it might not be worth it for an average weekend flyer.

On an aircraft that already has or was upgraded to a constant-speed propeller, additional modifications and options are available. The biggest change many owners consider making is switching from a two-blade to a three-blade propeller. Three-blade propeller systems are commonly billed as increasing aircraft speed, having more clearance from the ground, and being quieter. I can say that two of these—speed and clearance increases—are limited in terms of the real benefits gained.

The blades of three-blade propellers are only marginally shorter than the two-blade propellers that are on most general aviation aircraft. The effective clearance gained is marginal, and plus, if your propeller is going to strike the ground that probably means you have some other major problems occurring, such as a collapsed nose gear (on a tricycle gear aircraft) or a nose-over (on a tailwheel aircraft). The blade clearance may be the least of your concerns.

Three-blade propellers can provide a limited speed increase. Technically, two-blade propellers are more efficient than propellers with three or more blades. But, as engine horsepower increases, additional blades may be required to effectively use the power of the engine. It isn't just a speed thing; it's a balance of weight, engine power, and efficiency. An owner might have to really value the extra 5 knots of speed gained with a three-blade propeller to make the choice to switch. Keep in mind, for example, that an aircraft traveling 145 knots rather than 140 knots over the 953 miles from New York's LaGuardia Airport to Miami's airport will save only 14 minutes of flight time over the route. If you are thinking of changing your propeller to a three-blade system to "go faster," make sure your investment will provide enough of an increase in speed to be worth it. The improved speed may be marginally valuable.

One benefit of three-blade systems I can say I have personally noticed is that they are quieter than two-blade systems on the same airframe. This may have been of greater value to some owners before the availability of noise-canceling headsets than it is now. Whether you decide to make this change on your aircraft for this reason is based on personal comfort.

What about those weird propellers with the bent tips? Commonly referred to as Q-tip propellers, these do offer some performance improvements. An AOPA article accurately summarizes the benefits of Q-tip propellers:[3]

> The bent tips on a Q-tip propeller accomplish two things. First, the 90-degree bend acts like a wall to block air from flowing spanwise along the face of the blade (the side you see when sitting in the cockpit). On a normal straight blade this air mixes with air spilling off the camber side of the blade (the side you see when standing in front of the prop) to create tornado-like tip vortices. Aircraft wings also produce tip vortices when high-pressure air flowing spanwise across the cambered top of the wing mixes with lower-pressure air flowing spanwise across the flatter bottom of the wing. These wingtip vortices can produce potentially hazardous wake turbulence for following aircraft. Just as a winglet blocks tip vortices from forming off the end of an aircraft wing, a bent propeller tip blocks the formation of prop-tip vortices.
>
> The other main function of the Q-tip propeller is to reduce the diameter of the blade, typically by about two inches.
>
> Shrinking the blade's diameter and blocking the formation of tip vortices leads to several benefits. For one, the prop produces less noise. That's one reason Q-tip propellers are popular on aircraft in Europe, where noise restrictions are more stringent. Also, there's less chance the prop will stir up dust, dirt, and other foreign objects that can be sucked into the air cleaner or sent flying to strike another aircraft.

When it comes to my personal recommendation, I don't tell many owners to change a propeller system unless they are seeking to increase short-field performance, need to replace a damaged propeller, or need to overhaul a propeller for maintenance reasons. These are good times to make a change for owners who decide a different propeller will be worthwhile for their aircraft or situation.

---

3. Mark Twombly, "What it Looks Like When an Airplane Has a Q-Tip Propeller," Aircraft Owners and Pilots Association (AOPA) (website), Accessed October 10, 2019, https://www.aopa.org/asf/publications/inst_reports2.cfm?article=4060.

Another convenient opportunity to change a propeller system is at the time of an engine overhaul or change, although it can add cost to an already expensive process.

Expanding Fuel Capacity

Do you fly to places that have unreliable fuel availability? Are you a pilot who has an exceptional bladder and can make long-distance legs? If so, then perhaps you would like your aircraft to be able to carry more fuel.

Many aircraft can be modified to carry larger-capacity or more fuel tanks. The obvious benefit is that you can "tanker" fuel, allowing you to fly longer distances or to places where fuel may be difficult to secure and to which you otherwise might be unable to make a round trip without fueling. It can also provide a larger safety margin for alternate airports when operating in remote areas or areas where IFR conditions cover broad expanses.

The types of systems for expanding fuel capacity vary greatly. The easiest options offer increased sizes of tanks or bladders. The more complicated systems include installation of body tanks, wing tip tanks, changes to wings, or installation of tanks in the nacelle or baggage lockers. These will commonly require extra pumps to deliver the fuel from the extra tanks to the engine or to other tanks in the aircraft so the pilot can actually make use of the extra fuel. Nearly all types of expanded fuel systems will require the owner to have a maintenance provider modify the aircraft in accordance with an STC procedure.

The biggest problems that come with expanded fuel systems are the challenges of managing the systems and the obvious trade-off a pilot must make between carrying the weight of extra fuel and the passenger or baggage-carrying capacity. If we consider an example of a very basic four-person aircraft, this trade-off might be as shown in Figure 14.

4-Person Aircraft: Weight Comparison with Standard vs. Expanded Fuel	Weight (lbs)	
	Standard fuel	Expanded fuel
Gross weight	3,000	3,000
Empty weight	2,200	2,200
Standard fuel (50 gallons)	300	300
Additional fuel (50 gallons)		300
Total weight	2,500	2,800
Available excess capacity	500	200

Figure 14. Effect of expanded fuel on aircraft carrying capacity.

If you were flying the airplane in this simple example, you would be able to carry 500 pounds of people and baggage with the standard 50 gallons of fuel. However, if you took a full load of 100 gallons (with the expanded 50 gallons), it would certainly allow you to increase your range of operation, but the aircraft might only be able to take a pilot and no passengers!

If you are considering expanding your aircraft's fuel capacity, look at your normal operating loads of passengers and baggage and consider whether you will actually be able to carry more fuel even if you install additional tanks.

It is worth mentioning that enhanced fuel systems often add complexity to operations. You may need to burn some tanks down and then pump fuel into the main tanks from the supplemental tanks, or burn tanks in a specific order, when operating aircraft with modified fuel systems. If you are planning to modify your fuel system, make sure you know the operating limitations that will apply when the changes are completed.

It is also worth noting that adding fuel capacity doesn't typically increase gross weight allowances or landing weight limitations. It is easy in many aircraft—especially mid-sized, twin-engine aircraft—for pilots to find themselves in a situation where they have full fuel tanks, need to land, but are over a manufacturer-prescribed landing weight.

Figure 15 shows an example of how this might play out.

Maximum Landing Weight Consideration		
	Weight (lbs)	
	Standard fuel	Expanded fuel
Gross weight	6,000	6,000
Empty weight	4,000	4,000
Passengers (2)	400	400
Standard fuel (150 gallons)	900	900
Additional fuel (50 gallons)		300
Total fuel weight	900	1,200
Maximum landing weight	5,000	5,000
Total takeoff weight	5,300	5,600
Fuel burn per hour (gallons)	40	40
Weight required to burn to land	300	600
Fuel required to burn to land (gallons) *(weight required to burn to land ÷ 6)*	50	100
Flight time required to burn fuel to land (hours) *(Fuel required to burn to land ÷ fuel burn per hour)*	1.25	2.5

Figure 15. Effect of additional fuel on landing considerations.

In this example, that extra 50 gallons of fuel might allow the pilot to operate within takeoff limitations for weight and balance, but because the aircraft has a maximum landing weight of 5,000 pounds, the extra fuel load would require the pilot to fly an additional 1.25 hours (for a total of 2.5 hours) before being able to land!

Extra fuel adds extra weight, and the aircraft structure may not be capable of landing with this extra weight. This restriction is a common issue on many aircraft when extra fuel capacity is added, especially on aircraft with retractable gear.

Even when landing weights do not end up being a limiting factor, extra fuel means more weight, which means less weight capacity available for people or baggage. In most aircraft, there is a trade-off between people and fuel. Carefully consider what will be more important in your typical operations of your aircraft. That extra fuel may really only be useful when you are planning on flying longer legs. Or as another option, you could consider making additional modifications that will increase the gross weight of the aircraft to allow for both.

VGs for Gross Weight and Aerodynamic Performance

One of the most common and often easiest modifications many owners choose to make on their aircraft is installation of vortex generators (VGs) on the wings or other surfaces. VGs direct the airflow over the wing more efficiently and increase short-field and climb performance. In some cases, they also reduce stall speeds, allowing the aircraft to more safely operate at slower airspeeds, which can be critical during approach to landing.

VGs are little tabs that are glued to the wings and sometimes additionally to the tail surfaces. There are specifics for how and where to apply VGs, and if several go missing, any benefits may be nullified by the supplemental type certificate (STC). For many STC installations, if a few VGs fall off, the benefits gained by their installation may no longer be allowed to be utilized. Some care is warranted in maintaining VGs on the wing and making sure they do not break off, which most commonly occurs during a fueling operation when a hose is dragged across the wing.

VGs often offer an owner significant increases in gross weight allowances and enhance short-field takeoff performance. In many aircraft, the STC and installation of these VGs allow the use of new performance charts for shorter takeoff distances. VGs don't allow for increases in landing weights, but the difference in maximum takeoff weight can be significant. In many cases, the differences are hundreds of pounds, which can equate to an extra passenger or two or an extra 50 gallons of fuel in the auxiliary tanks an owner installed.

The installation of VGs is a great modification for an owner to consider for an aircraft to improve its load-hauling utility and for adding a safety margin when it comes to actual aircraft takeoff, landing, and stalling performance.

Short-Field Performance

Being able to get an aircraft in and out of shorter fields holds a certain appeal for some owners. Not every aircraft will be one you can fly into a gravel bar 50 miles from civilization in Alaska, but even modest performance increases can be achieved with modifications for grass fields, shorter paved runways, or airports that have nearby obstacles.

We already discussed some changes—such as bigger engines, different propellers, and VGs—that can help with short-field performance, but there are also other modifications that can help.

Some aircraft have wing tips available for purchase that modify how the airflow transitions out the end of the wing. These wing tips help direct the airflow more efficiently and increase short-field performance. These are most common on aircraft that have metal wings and removable wing tips, such as single-engine Cessna and Piper aircraft, but they may also be available for other models. This can be a quick modification with easy installation.

Flap modifications are also possible on many aircraft. Flaps that can be extended more degrees on landing can provide lower stall speeds that can allow a pilot to approach at lower speeds for shorter landing rolls. While these won't help much during takeoff, it can make a landing much safer on short fields if the takeoff is not the main concern.

Improvements for Rough Backcountry Flying

Many of the modifications discussed above are common on aircraft that are used in grass, gravel, or even unimproved runway conditions. For owners planning on using their aircraft in even more specialized or backcountry conditions, more options can be added to the mix.

Removing wheel pants, adding bigger or even bald tundra tires, bigger tail wheels, clear door panels, and any number of other unique modifications can take an aircraft to the next level. If you are planning on moving to a remote cabin on an island in the Bahamas where there is only a 1,000-foot-long, crushed coral runway, it might be time to find an airframe to modify as much as possible.

These modifications do come with some limitations. Bigger and bald tundra tires cut into cruise speed and don't last for as many landings on pavement. Before you make your aircraft a backcountry beast, consider whether you are really going to use it for that purpose. The backcountry modifications may look pretty cool to you, but in some cases, they could actually increase your cost of operations for the aircraft over the long term for something you will not even really use. If you are going to modify your aircraft, build it up to do what you will be using it for.

Some aircraft makes and models tend to have many more modifications approved and available for them than others. Aircraft such as the Cessna 180 that are commonly used as backcountry aircraft have many potential modifications that can be made. A die-hard owner looking to make the most of an airframe might put a constant-speed three-blade prop, droop wing tips, big tundra tires, a monster of an engine, VGs, and extra fuel tanks all on the same aircraft in an effort to build a true short-field, backcountry aircraft. This can completely change the utility and performance of the aircraft compared to how it was originally delivered. The same will not necessarily be possible with an owner's two-year-old Cirrus SR22 for which this range of modifications is not available. But if modifications are available for your airframe, it is to some degree a personal decision whether to implement them and how much investment you want to make in the aircraft.

Multiple Weight and Balance Documents

A common "upgrade" that many owners choose and that doesn't require overly expensive changes is to have multiple weight and balance documents approved for their aircraft. This is common for aircraft that have more seats than can typically be filled with people due to weight and balance considerations. Removing seats can provide more physical space for baggage or gear, easier entry into the aircraft, and some limited benefits for weight and balance.

For example, the owner of a Cessna 206 who typically flies with only the pilot and one passenger may choose to remove the four rear seats in the aircraft. If we assume each seat weighs 30 pounds, this change could provide overall weight benefits as shown in Figure 16.

Cessna 206	Weight (lbs)	
	Original (6 seats)	With removal of 4 seats
Gross weight	3,300	3,300
Empty weight	2,000	2,000
Standard fuel (65 gallons)	390	390
Removal of 4 rear seats		−120
Total weight	2,390	2,270
Available excess capacity	910	1,030

Figure 16. Changes in excess weight capacity with the removal of seats in a Cessna 206.

Although it may not seem like a significant change to be able to carry an extra 120 pounds of payload, in many cases it could allow the aircraft to take a couple extra bags or a small passenger.

You may ask, "Can't I just remove the seats and not worry about doing a new weight and balance?" The official answer is, no. When considering weight and balance, removing seats will not only remove weight in the cabin but will also change the center of gravity for the aircraft, albeit typically not significantly. So, if you plan to operate with any of the seats removed, the best practice is to have your maintenance professional calculate and sign-off a weight and balance for the aircraft that represents its configuration with those seats removed.

There is certainly nothing wrong with having multiple weight and balance documents for an aircraft. I know many operators who have different weight and balance documents to represent their aircraft in multiple configurations. An owner of a Beechcraft Baron BE55 may choose to have both a six-seat and a five-seat weight and balance; a Cessna 210 owner may choose to have only a four-seat weight and balance configuration since the rear two seats are quite small and never used by many owners; and the owner of a Cessna 172 on floats may choose to remove the back seats and only operate the aircraft using a two-seat weight and balance configuration.

. . .

Deciding whether to make modifications really comes down to what you are trying to do with your aircraft. If you will only be using 4,000-foot-long, paved runways, modifying your aircraft with tundra tires may be something you think looks cool, but it probably will not be worth the investment. If you will be flying only within a 200-mile radius, adding enough fuel tanks to fly 7½ hours and flying with them full will just cut into your useful load without really making any functional difference in the utility of your aircraft. But if your aircraft can be modified to increase the possibilities for your intended operations or improve safety, consider and evaluate potential modifications to see if they will enhance the aircraft's performance or increase its utility.

No matter what type or number of modifications you are considering, it is worth looking at the benefits that will be gained and balancing these against the limitations and costs that will result.

I'll wrap this up with a reminder that your aircraft is not like a Jeep that you can tinker with on your own. If you are not a licensed and experienced A&P and/or IA mechanic, or unless your aircraft is an experimental aircraft and you are an experienced builder, don't do these modifications on your own. Get qualified help and ensure they are done the right way.

Chapter 17

Avionics Upgrades

Is It Time to Upgrade Avionics?

Many pilots want to upgrade the avionics in their aircraft, but whether upgrading is really necessary is an entirely different question. Any aircraft owner would love to have the latest, coolest, and most capable equipment, but that comes at a cost—often a very high cost.

In many cases, aircraft owners don't really *need* an avionics upgrade, they just *want* to upgrade. Based on my experiences, I have concluded that there are four different reasons to complete an avionics upgrade: to replace broken equipment, to increase capability, to enhance safety, or simply because of desire.

Upgrading to Replace Broken Equipment

No matter how well we try to take care of our aircraft, as they get older, parts and components break. Or perhaps some avionics devices were already broken when an aircraft was purchased. In either case, the owner must decide whether to replace the equipment with a like piece or take the opportunity to upgrade it. When replacing broken equipment, that can be the right time to make upgrades to newer, more capable equipment, even though doing so may cost more money than a simple replacement. The cost of buying replacement equipment and then also paying to upgrade it later can result in greater long-term costs than taking the opportunity to make upgrades when the equipment initially breaks.

Upgrading to Increase Capability

Do you have an old stack of avionics that doesn't allow you to fly all the approaches you might need? If so, then it might be time for an upgrade. An aircraft with two VORs, no DME, and an ADF is hard to even call IFR-capable anymore. The modern IFR system relies heavily on GPS navigation systems and less on VORs and DME data than ever before, and NDB approaches are almost gone in most areas.

Upgrading an old panel to give an aircraft the capability of flying more modern approaches increases the ability of the aircraft (and a properly trained pilot) to fly to more destinations and fly in more challenging weather conditions. A WAAS-capable GPS can take a pilot even further with the enhanced aircraft capabilities. An avionics upgrade justified for its increase in aircraft capability can also lead to an increase in the overall utility of the aircraft for a pilot. This can be extremely valuable, especially to a business traveler.

Upgrading to Enhance Safety

Avionics upgrades can lead to enhanced safety. Adding a quality autopilot can help workload management for a pilot flying in single-pilot IFR conditions. Adding onboard weather data (satellite or ADS-B based) can increase pilots' awareness of weather conditions ahead and allow them to make earlier decisions in order to avoid potentially dangerous or unforecast weather. Adding digital fuel or engine monitoring gauges can significantly increase a pilot's awareness of engine parameters and fuel consumption compared with older analog gauges.

It's important to mention that new "gadgets" in the cockpit have the potential to cause distractions for the pilot; however, when properly used by a trained pilot, these instruments can enhance safety in flight operations through improved awareness and by providing much more detailed information on aircraft control.

Upgrading Because of Desire

In some cases, there is not a real "need" to upgrade, but the owner may simply want to. There is nothing wrong with completing an upgrade for this reason. If everything we did in life had to be completely justified by a practical application, then chasing a golf ball around a course and hitting it with a stick would probably never have become a sport. We do it because we choose to.

You may upgrade your aircraft's avionics for the same reason. An old, round gauge ILS may get you to the same point on the same ILS as a new, digital GPS unit, but perhaps you would like to have the newer unit that looks much prettier in the panel. It's OK. I give you permission to make an upgrade such as this if your budget allows. But be honest with yourself about the reasons when you make an upgrade under these conditions. Are you doing it because you are trying to justify a true need or just because you would prefer to have the newer equipment in your aircraft's panel?

Downgrading as an Upgrade

A less commonly considered option is to downgrade the instruments in your aircraft. This may sound counterintuitive at first, but if you have an older aircraft with multiple pieces of equipment that no longer work and you don't have the budget to upgrade or replace the equipment, it might make sense to remove the non-working equipment entirely if it isn't required.

For example, the next time you bring your aircraft in for an annual, you could ask the IA mechanic to remove that old ADF that hasn't worked for a decade and the rotary DME that locked up five years ago. If you still have a LORAN in the panel, it can also probably be removed. The reality is that if you have multiple instruments in your panel that no longer work, you may be tempted to fly IFR with less equipment than you should be utilizing to be safe. Although removing this equipment may "downgrade" your aircraft to a strictly VFR machine, it also may remove your temptation to work through marginally IFR conditions when your aircraft really should not be flying in IFR conditions anymore. If you don't fly IFR, you may not even miss this old, dead equipment.

Removing non-functional equipment may also reduce electrical loads on older alternators, remove the potential for electrical shorts caused by unused equipment, and as an added bonus, give you back a little of the useful load for the aircraft. You might be surprised how many pounds an ADF, a LORAN, and a dead NAV/COM and the associated wiring can add up to in weight, and removing it could allow you to take along an extra grandchild for a Saturday afternoon flight.

When you are thinking of upgrading instruments in your aircraft, it is always worth considering what your reasons are for doing so. In many cases when I have had this discussion with fellow pilots and clients of mine, the conclusion has been that no upgrade is really needed. If you are considering an upgrade that will not enhance your safety, increase the capability of your aircraft to fly new or more complex procedures, or replace broken equipment, perhaps there really is no need to complete the upgrade. That is, of course, unless you have considered all of this and still just want to. And that's OK, too, as long as you are honest with yourself about the real motivation to make the changes.

Chapter 18

The Engine Overhaul or Swap

Most engines have a recommended period of time—measured either in years or more commonly usage hours—at which point the manufacturer suggests that the engine be overhauled.

But when should you really do an engine overhaul? Or when should you put a new engine in the aircraft? Or can you perhaps just change the cylinders and get some more operational time from the engine?

If your aircraft's engine has reached its TBO point and is getting up there in its total time, should you buy a new one or have the factory overhaul it? Should you call a commercial, non-manufacturer overhauler or have the local mechanic do the work?

These questions are hotly debated in the general aviation community, and the answers vary wildly. To some degree, the decisions are up to the owners of the aircraft and their willingness to take risks. Each of these options comes with different risks.

Let's start with the first question.

When Should You Change or Overhaul an Aircraft Engine?

How do you know when you need to change or overhaul your aircraft's engine? The simple answer is, when something is wrong enough that it cannot be fixed without replacement or overhaul.

A manufacturer's recommended time between overhauls (TBO) is more about risk and liability than it is a belief by the manufacturer that the engine will suddenly fail after a specific number of hours of engine usage or span of time. Manufacturers must set a time somewhere that they are willing to accept, and in many cases, the TBO is conservative. Unless you will be operating your aircraft in a commercial endeavor, these overhaul recommendations are typically non-mandatory (unless an AD applies, for example).

A statement by well-known general aviation maintenance professional Mike Busch is worth sharing here. In an AOPA article, "The Dark Side of Maintenance," Mike notes that,[4]

> Maintenance has a dark side that isn't usually discussed in polite company. It sometimes breaks aircraft instead of fixing them.

This certainly applies to a significant degree when it comes to aircraft engines. Mike takes this approach much further in his book, *Manifesto: A Revolutionary Approach to General Aviation Maintenance*, applying it to all aircraft maintenance.[5] It is a book that I encourage all aircraft owners to read to help determine the best approach to maintenance on their own aircraft.

And specifically relating to engine overhaul times, one of Busch's articles on AVweb entitled "The Savvy Aviator #4: Debunking TBO"[6] focuses on the myth of the "required" TBO of an aircraft engine. In this article, he lays out the statistical, data-based case for the reality of the safety of operation of an aircraft beyond a manufacturer's recommended TBO when the aircraft is being properly maintained. It even highlights the fact that operations past the recommended TBO may be less risky than those during the first hours on an engine after an overhaul or installation of a new engine. This article is worth the read.

An engine that has recently had an overhaul has been taken fully apart and put back together. The goal of this process is to make certain all parts are within specifications and that the engine will run nearly as well as it did when it was new. But the fact remains

---

4. Mike Busch, "The Dark Side of Maintenance," AOPA, June 10, 2014, https://blog.aopa.org/aopa/2014/06/10/dark-side-of-maintenance/

5. Mike Busch, *Manifesto: A Revolutionary Approach to General Aviation Maintenance* (Las Vegas: Savvy Aviator, Inc., 2014).

6. Mike Busch, "The Savvy Aviator #4: Debunking TBO," AVweb, April 14, 2004, https://www.avweb.com/ownership/the-savvy-aviator-4-debunking-tbo/.

that a just-overhauled engine was recently taken apart. Any time something is taken apart, there is the potential for human error in putting it back together. Statistical data indicates that the first couple hundred hours after an engine overhaul are actually more likely to experience a failure than even the 500 hours beyond a manufacturer's recommended overhaul time!

An engine that is three-quarters of the way through its recommended time between overhauls but that has had a new "top" (cylinders) installed on it and has been actively flown a couple of hundred hours a year will probably prove to be a good bet and work well beyond its overhaul period. In comparison, a low-time engine that was last overhauled two decades ago, has not had new cylinders installed, and has been flown only 10 hours in the last 5 years is likely to start developing problems if you start operating it regularly. For example, seals dry out and crack and cylinders develop corrosion when they are not used, to name only a few of the potential concerns. The best thing for an aircraft engine is for it to be operated on a regular basis.

So, with that in mind, if your mechanic is telling you that you really must overhaul your aircraft's engine or swap it out with a new one—but everything is still running fine, you are still getting good compressions, there aren't any cracks in the cylinders or the case, and it isn't leaking anywhere—then you might want to get another opinion. Deciding just how far you go beyond a recommended overhaul becomes partly a matter of personal comfort, and it should be based more on the continued tracking of the aircraft engine condition than on an arbitrary number.

Considerations When Completing an Engine Swap or Overhaul

At some point in your aircraft ownership, you will probably have an aircraft that does need something done about its "tired" engine. When it does come time to swap or overhaul an engine, you will have some decisions to make.

The first question will be whether to keep your current engine and have it overhauled or swap it out for a different engine that is new or has been newly overhauled. Swapping your engine and getting a core deposit value might not be an available option if you are in need of an engine because the case of yours was damaged and no longer serviceable. But if that isn't the case, you have a decision to make.

There are potential benefits and risks with both options, keeping your engine components or switching to an all-new engine. Switching engines to a "crated" engine can often result in a faster process because you can preplan to have the new engine available when your maintenance shop is scheduled to install it. The risk is that you will be getting a "new-to-you" engine rather than one for which you may know a long, detailed history and which requires only an overhaul. It is probably good to have a discussion with your maintenance provider when carefully considering this decision. Many owners like to get their own case and components back from an overhaul, choosing to go with the devil they know instead of potentially introducing a new one. If you have the time to wait for an overhaul and deal with the downtime of the aircraft, that option may be what you choose.

If you decide to swap your engine, you may choose to get one from an overhauler shop that has one in stock or perhaps from a manufacturer who overhauls engines back within factory standards. In some cases, you may be able to get a factory-new engine that has never been installed on any other aircraft. Understanding each of these options can be important in making a knowledgeable decision.

A factory-overhauled engine does not necessarily mean that the engine is new. It just means that it has been overhauled to be within the factory specifications that allow a "zero-time" engine to be issued. This can be done on engines that have been previously installed on an aircraft but are then later overhauled. These engines are not necessarily any better than what you would get from a good overhauler shop, which also can "zero-time" an engine during an overhaul.

Many overhauler shops do wonderful work, and sometimes they specialize in aircraft engines that factories are no longer building new. In these cases, an overhauler shop may be the best, most experienced, and most reliable provider of the engine that will best fit your aircraft.

Even factory-new engines have some downsides. Their biggest drawback is that they may be the most expensive. In addition, engine manufacturers are not necessarily still making all engines. If you are purchasing an engine that is currently in production and that is being used on aircraft currently in production, you will probably get a great product. But if you ask a manufacturer to make an engine that it has not made in twenty years, it will probably be willing to do it but may no longer have staff who are as familiar with the details of that model. I have seen a couple of these engines, from multiple different manufacturers, turn out to be full of "bugs" that end up taking time and expense to solve.

If you decide to have your aircraft's engine overhauled and wait as it is removed, shipped out, and overhauled instead of just swapping for another engine already completed, an equally important decision is who you choose to complete the work. Your average mechanic at the local airport FBO probably does not typically do engine overhauls. In that case, it might make sense to allow a shop that specializes in that work to do the actual overhaul while the local FBO mechanic handles the engine removal and replacement after the overhaul is completed. Overhauling engines takes specialty equipment, knowledge of the process, and in some cases, contacts for specific parts that make the process go more quickly and smoothly.

Not every engine overhaul is the same quality. I have seen some cases in which engines overhauled in large, spotless shops have turned out to be really bad work, while other times, engine overhauls completed by providers on dirt-floored hangars have been of impeccable quality and lasted well beyond recommended TBOs. And sometimes the opposites are true.

Therefore, it is important to do your homework. Ask for references from the shop you are considering, and talk with those references. Anyone can have maintenance problems occur, but if there is a pattern of repeated problems with work done by a specific shop, look elsewhere. It is also important to ask how long the overhaul will take. Some great shops have long wait lists for engine overhauls. But in some cases, it can be worth the wait.

There are no right or wrong answers to these questions, but it's definitely worth thinking through the factors discussed above. The best decisions will balance all the factors such as price, how long you are willing to wait, what providers are available that are experienced with the engine you are managing, and what level of risk you feel comfortable taking.

Remember that if your aircraft's engine quits, it gets pretty quiet and the range you can travel becomes limited to how far you can glide. The cheapest engine work you can find may not be the choice that will serve your flying needs safely for the longest period of time. Your life may depend on the choices you make when it comes time to overhaul or swap the engine on your aircraft.

Chapter 19

Planning and Budgeting for Future Maintenance

An aircraft will not last forever without maintenance. In addition to typical operating expenses such as annual inspections, fuel usage, and hangar and insurance costs, a savvy owner will also plan for future maintenance expenses. It is important for aircraft owners to understand what these costs will amount to over time as well as how they might affect an aircraft's actual hourly operating costs.

Chapter 1 showed an example of how to calculate aircraft expenses per hour of operation taking into account standard variable and fixed costs and also including basic reserve costs for engine and propeller overhauls, as well as unexpected maintenance needs. In this chapter, I use a different example aircraft to demonstrate some of these same hourly operating expenses but also expand it to include the costs of potential future upgrades. This can help you determine the aircraft's maintenance cost footprint over the course of a year or longer period to assist in planning and budgeting. Looking at different specific examples such as these can be helpful in gaining a full understanding of what total ownership and operation costs might look like for your aircraft.

Major expenses that an owner should plan for over time include engine overhauls, propeller overhauls, and avionics service. It is also a great idea to plan for some general maintenance expenses that will occur as the aircraft is operated. Annual inspections will not always come out completely clean (some items may need to be repaired or replaced) and not every flight in between those annuals will be completed without something breaking. Certainly, every owner's hope is that the aircraft will operate with a normal cost footprint without encountering any major surprise problems. But even if this is the case, there are some unavoidable expenses that occur over time.

With that in mind, let's put into perspective how some of these costs may affect the hourly operating footprint of an aircraft.

Understanding that the engine on an aircraft will eventually need to be overhauled, let's start with an example of an aircraft engine that is relatively new, with only 50 hours of operation since its last overhaul and a 2,000-hour, manufacturer-recommended time between overhauls. If we expect the overhaul with a removal and reinstall to cost $25,000, we can calculate the hourly reserve cost of operation for that engine, assuming nothing else goes wrong at all, as shown in Figure 17.

Engine Reserve Calculation		Description
Current engine time (SMOH)	50 hours	The current engine tach time (SMOH = since major overhaul).
Time between overhauls (TBO)	2,000 hours	The manufacturer's recommended TBO hours for the engine, or a time that you expect it will need to be completed.
Flight time to engine overhaul	1,950 hours	The expected remaining hours able to be flown until an engine overhaul is required.
Estimated engine overhaul cost	$25,000	The expected cost of an overhaul or replacement of the engine, including the engine and all labor.
Engine hourly reserve required	**$12.82**	The hourly reserve amount to save to allow the engine to be overhauled or replaced when due under normal conditions.

Figure 17. Calculation of engine reserve required per hour of operation.

This $12.82 calculated above is just a basic engine reserve that the owner might consider as representing the operating cost of that engine on a basic single-engine aircraft. If the aircraft has two engines, this amount should be doubled.

Next, let's look at a similar required hourly reserve calculation for a propeller on the same aircraft using the same assumptions. A common fixed-pitch propeller on a single-engine aircraft might result in math as shown in Figure 18.

Propeller Reserve Calculation		Description
Current propeller time (SMOH)	50 hours	The current propeller tach time.
Time between overhauls (TBO)	2,000 hours	The manufacturer's recommended TBO hours for the propeller, or the time interval that you expect it will need to be completed.
Flight time to propeller overhaul	1,950 hours	The expected remaining hours able to be flown until a propeller overhaul is required.
Estimated propeller overhaul cost	$5,000	The expected cost of an overhaul or replacement of the propeller, including the propeller and all labor.
Propeller hourly reserve required	**$2.56**	The hourly reserve that must be saved to allow the propeller to be overhauled or replaced when due under normal conditions.

Figure 18. Calculation of propeller reserve required per hour of operation.

Although a whopping $2.56 might not seem like much, every dollar adds up, as will become more apparent as we continue through this exercise.

Next, let's consider an additional amount to put aside for costs relating to the rest of the airframe, the avionics, and a broad general category. Tires wear out, hoses get chafed, dents happen, cracks appear, and brakes need replacing. Even a modest allocation per hour of operation for these types of considerations might look like Figure 19.

General Reserve Costs to Allocate		Description
Airframe	$5.00	The expected general airframe reserve per hour of flight to accommodate for any airframe maintenance beyond the cost of annual inspections.
Avionics	$5.00	The expected general avionics reserve per hour of flight to cover expected or possible avionics upgrades, or replacement of items due to wear and tear.
General	$5.00	The expected general overall aircraft reserve per hour of flight to accommodate for any airframe maintenance (not covered under the other categories above) beyond the cost of typical annual inspections.
Total per-hour allocation for general reserve	**$15.00**	

Figure 19. Calculation of general reserve allocation per hour of operation.

If we total all these maintenance reserve costs, the result is an hourly operating maintenance reserve that could be considered representative of this example aircraft, as follows:

Engine hourly reserve:	$12.82
Propeller hourly reserve:	$2.56
General hourly reserve:	$15.00
Total per hour reserve required for normal operations:	**$30.38**

This $30.38 does not include any other costs such as fuel, insurance, or hangar expenses associated with operating an aircraft. This reserve is just the amount that an owner might need to put aside for every hour flown in order to keep the aircraft flying.

To put this in perspective, over the expected 1,950 hours of operation remaining before the engine and propeller would be overhauled or replaced, the owner would need to put aside $59,241. In many cases, this maintenance allocation may actually be more total money than the initial acquisition cost of the aircraft!

It becomes even worse if we take it a step further and consider other potential maintenance or upgrades.

Do you think there is a major upgrade of avionics in your aircraft's future? If you plan to complete this upgrade in two years after 500 hours of flying, Figure 20 shows the hourly reserve that will be required.

Planned Avionics Upgrade		Description
Expected cost	$30,000	The expected cost of the upgrade.
Flight time until completed	500 hours	The number of hours of operation until the owner plans to complete the upgrade.
Total hourly reserve required	**$60**	

Figure 20. Calculation of reserve required per hour of operation for planned avionics upgrades.

Or perhaps you're planning to get a new aircraft paint job. Similarly assuming you will have this completed after 500 more hours of flying, that paint job might have a cost footprint as shown in Figure 21.

Paint Job		Description
Expected cost	$20,000	The expected cost for the paint job.
Flight time until completed	500 hours	The number of hours of operation until the owner plans to complete the work.
Total hourly reserve required	**$40**	

Figure 21. Calculation of reserve required per hour of operation for future paint job.

And if you are going to have a new paint job done on the aircraft, how about also refurbishing or replacing the interior? Spread across the same 500 hours of flying, that interior work would have an hourly cost footprint as shown in Figure 22.

Interior Refurbishment		Description
Expected cost	$10,000	The expected cost for the interior work.
Flight time until completed	500 hours	The number of hours of operation until the owner plans to complete the work.
Total hourly reserve required	**$20**	

Figure 22. Calculation of reserve required per hour of operation for future interior refurbishment.

Putting this all together, if we consider the previously calculated per-hour maintenance reserves over the next 500 hours of operation along with the additional upgrades planned, the total hourly operating maintenance reserve would be as shown below.

Normal operations hourly reserve (engine, propeller, and general reserves):	$30.38
Avionics upgrade hourly reserve:	$60.00
New paint job hourly reserve:	$40.00
Interior refurbishment hourly reserve:	$20.00
Total new reserve needed per hour of operation if upgrades are planned:	**$150.38**

Making this seem even worse, if we look at what it would amount to in terms of a yearly cost footprint considering different possible numbers of hours of operation per year, the expected reserve costs would be as follows:

Hours of Operation	**Required Yearly Reserve**
100 hours/year	$15,038.46
200 hours/year	$30,076.92
300 hours/year	$45,115.38

Adding this all together—the planned upgrades completed after 500 hours ($120 × 500 = $60,000) and reserve costs for normal operations over the full 1,950 hours ($30.38 × 1,950)—the total amount would come to $119,241 to keep the aircraft flying, replace the engine, overhaul the propeller, and do the avionics, paint job, and interior work. If you do these calculations on an aircraft such as a Piper Cherokee that might be valued at $60,000 in the end, the costs can become a major consideration in deciding whether to do these upgrades when they come due or instead go buy a different aircraft.

These are big numbers, but it does not mean I am trying to scare anyone away from aircraft ownership. However, it's important for owners to have a realistic understanding of the costs so they don't find themselves unable to keep an aircraft flying simply because they didn't budget for the expenses that will be encountered.

Although the total costs will vary, I strongly encourage owners to understand the real operating footprint of an aircraft and to plan and budget for more long-term maintenance needs or desires. An owner who is planning ahead might choose to put these reserve funds aside in an account throughout the years of operation of the aircraft so that the funds are ready and available when maintenance is needed. At the least, an owner should understand that these maintenance costs will be encountered at some point and include them in the real costs of operating the aircraft over time. Having accurate knowledge of the actual operating costs including maintenance reserve costs will help owners budget for future cost expectations over the duration of their aircraft operations.

Do you want a good idea of how this might apply to your aircraft with different calculations? To assist with this, I created a personal aircraft operating cost calculator spreadsheet that you can modify and update with your aircraft's specifics to get a realistic picture of the real budgetary concerns that you may experience relating to your own aircraft. (See the online Reader Resources at www.asa2fly.com/reader/avown.)

Chapter 20

Throwaway Planes?

Some planes are probably not worth reinvesting in when major components require replacement or overhaul. In a sense, the high cost of doing this work will make an owner have to consider whether to instead "throw away" the aircraft.

Older aircraft may now be considered disposable items. This is probably counterintuitive to what most pilots and aircraft owners have been accustomed to in the past, but it can be argued to be true in many cases. What do I mean by disposable? I mean, for example, that an owner of an older aircraft may at some point no longer find the aircraft valuable enough that it makes sense to replace or overhaul the engine when it is timed out and the work is required.

I know that this probably seems blasphemous to many owners. I don't necessarily mean that the aircraft should be given to the local scrap yard and crushed. But owners may find that it makes better financial sense to part the aircraft out instead of putting it back together as a fully airworthy, marketable aircraft.

If you own a 1951 V-tail Beechcraft Bonanza that needs a new engine, you may discover that the cost of that new engine could quickly exceed $30,000 or even $40,000. If you originally paid $60,000 for the aircraft, that means you might have invested nearly $100,000 into the wonderful old V-tail but perhaps could sell it only for the same price you paid for it—or worse, less. You can get financially upside down on some aircraft when major maintenance is needed. In these cases, it just might not be worth putting money into an aircraft that won't be worth more on the market when the work is completed. In a many instances, you could literally throw the aircraft away, go buy another one of the same style, and be money ahead compared to if you had paid for the major maintenance. This is becoming more common with older aircraft.

When owners really consider all the costs of ownership related to the aircraft itself (excluding things like insurance, hangar, general maintenance costs, GPS subscriptions, etc.), the math may actually show that the owners would come out ahead if they just bought another of the same make and model of aircraft with lower-time engines or upgrades already completed. If you get to this point, I am not saying that you shouldn't get anything at all for your aircraft. You may be able to part it out, sell it for a bargain price and use the proceeds as a deposit on another aircraft, or even donate it for a tax write-off and end up "money ahead" with all things considered. Owners who spend the money to overhaul engines, put in new interiors, or upgrade avionics never get their full invested value back in a marketable sale price. The same will hold true of an aircraft you intend to do this with. It may be time for you to think about letting someone take that hit on the value of their aircraft and just dump your aircraft, take what you can get out of it, and go buy something else. Seriously—if you get to this point, do the math.

This necessarily brings the question up, "So, when *should* I invest back in an aircraft that needs an overhaul or upgrades?"

The answer to that question is not a financial one. Pure math will almost never show that investment in the aircraft would be cheaper than buying a like-equipped aircraft available for sale. However, that doesn't mean you will never decide to reinvest in your aircraft. Choosing to do overhauls or upgrades may be based on personal or market reasons or the lack of availability for purchase of an aircraft that "has all you want" already installed, refurbished, or overhauled. For example, perhaps your aircraft was your grandfather's aircraft or has been in your family for years and holds sentimental value that makes you want to hold on to it and keep using it. Or maybe you own an aircraft for which it would currently be difficult to find a replacement on the used market. If these or other personal reasons apply to your case, then you might make the decision to overhaul, update, or upgrade the aircraft not only based purely on whether it makes financial sense. Make such a decision mindfully.

Sometimes the concept of "good guts" applies. For example, this may be true in cases where you have a known aircraft that you may have owned for quite some time, and you have already "worked out the bugs" in it and only need to upgrade, overhaul, or refurbish some parts or components. Dumping your current aircraft and starting fresh on the process of working the bugs out of a different aircraft will come with some risks—the unknown potential problems that the new aircraft may have. Even if it might be cheaper to do so, confidence in a particular aircraft—not just the make and model but the specific, tail-numbered aircraft—may in itself make reinvesting in the aircraft worthwhile, even if the cost of a new engine on it might be more expensive.

There are intrinsic values that are hard to put a price on, but if the aircraft is just a tool for you to "get there," there might be more economical options to meet that need.

Chapter 21

Selling Your Aircraft

Any book that discusses buying or owning an aircraft would be remiss if it did not also at least briefly cover the subject of selling an aircraft. People may decide to sell their aircraft for many reasons, including wanting to upgrade, changing personal or family budget considerations, losing a medical, or just changing hobbies. Whatever the reason, a little knowledge about the process can go a long way toward selling your aircraft for a better price or in a timelier manner.

It can even be worth considering some of these points before you buy an aircraft! If you know you are only going to keep an aircraft for a limited time, you may choose to purchase an aircraft that can be easily resold. For example, if your three children are in high school and will soon be leaving your parental nest, you may decide that you need a Cherokee 6 with six seats for a few years but then will only need a two-seat aircraft, since it will only be you and your spouse traveling after the kids move on to college. This may be a reason to own a larger plane now while planning to change in a few years to one with fewer seats that may be a bit sportier. In a case like this, buying an aircraft that is easily insurable and for which there is available maintenance and readily available parts may be a good choice because there will be a bigger buyer's market when you go to sell it. There are reasons some aircraft hold their value for decades. If you buy an aircraft that is hard to maintain or is not very popular or common, this can limit the potential future market. So, it is a good idea to think about this ahead of time if possible.

With that in mind, if you already have an aircraft that you are planning to sell, there are some things that you can do to make a sale process go smoother.

First, since you are reading this, you might be aware of another one of my books, *An Aviator's Field Guide to Buying an Aircraft*. That book is designed to help potential buyers through the process of finding and buying an aircraft. This chapter focuses on what you can do on the other side of the equation when selling—how to increase the chances that buyers will be interested in buying your aircraft and how to list and market it so potential buyers can find it.

The first thing to do is to prep the aircraft for a sale. Do everything you can to make it mechanically sound, aesthetically appealing, and informationally complete. Get a good annual inspection done. Clean the aircraft. And ensure you have information and paperwork for the aircraft collected and organized. I provide specific tips later in this chapter that highlight commonly overlooked considerations. Properly preparing for a sale will go a long way toward ensuring you are ready to field calls, inquiries, and visits from potential buyers. Thus, it is important to complete this step before you list your aircraft anywhere.

To avoid any hiccups in the sale process, do some of the homework that a buyer might do. It might sound stupid, but do a lien check on your own aircraft. I have seen multiple cases in which an owner wasn't aware of a 30-year-old lien from a bank that is not even in business anymore and that did not properly execute a lien release from a previous owner when a loan was paid off. Check this ahead of time so a potential buyer doesn't find it when they do a title search. Having a clear title and ability to sell an aircraft is likely to be a contingency for a buyer's purchase if they are going to finance the aircraft. If you find a lien, get it cleared before you have to deal with it while the closing of a sale is pending with a buyer.

Paperwork is important in the sale process. Make sure your registration (federal and state, if applicable) is current. Make sure the aircraft has a current (and legible) airworthiness certificate or get a replacement copy from the FAA. And make sure the required documents for the aircraft are all present, such as the POH, supplements, and the weight and balance (one that is current and that represents the current configuration of the aircraft). I know this all sounds simple, but I have very frequently seen these items missing when an owner is trying to sell an aircraft.

Once you have completed this prep work, think about how you want to sell your aircraft. Do you want to do it personally, or do you want to have a broker do it for you?

Using a Broker

The benefit to selling an aircraft yourself is that you will not have to pay a commission to the broker in the sale. The disadvantage is you must do all the work yourself.

A broker can serve as a buffer between you and all the tire-kicker calls that surely will come in a sale process. Brokers will often have a customer base that may already include potential buyers, and a good broker will be knowledgeable about the market. If you get a good broker, it can help the sale go more quickly and smoothly.

Carefully review any sales contracts up front, be knowledgeable about any commissions, and be willing to ask questions before giving a broker the listing of your aircraft. Interview a couple of brokers so you can compare them and pick the one that best meets your needs.

Good brokers will be familiar with the market and can advise you on what to expect for a good listing price and realistic sales price. The good news is that when brokers are working on a commission that is based on a percentage of the sales price, they are often as motivated as the seller to get a high asking price for the aircraft. Remember, a broker acts as your agent in the sale, not as an agent for the buyer. Make an agent be exactly that.

In the broker selection process, ask how they plan to market the aircraft. Will they only list it on one website? Do they have a customer database from years of working within the industry? I know one aircraft maintenance shop that works with many Beechcraft owners and regularly brokers their aircraft. When I have a customer looking for a good A36 Bonanza or Baron, I typically call this shop first because I know they are very knowledgeable about the market and often know owners who may be willing to sell great aircraft.

When you are looking for a broker, find one who is knowledgeable about the type of aircraft are selling. If you are trying to sell your Cessna 210, a jet broker who specializes in Learjets probably won't do the best job for you.

The right broker may not be within 25 miles of your hometown or even in the same state. Remember that these are airplanes, and they can fly across the country. Don't limit yourself to only considering the broker closest to where you live. If you own a late-model Mooney aircraft in North Carolina, you may discover a broker who specializes in these aircraft located in Texas. That doesn't mean the broker can't be a good listing agent for you. However, using a distant broker will probably require you to do more work to provide information and help coordinate potential buyer showings than if the aircraft and buyers are in the same location. Nevertheless, a broker who is not in your area may be the best option for the market. As an alternative, you may choose to relocate your aircraft to the broker's location so they can handle the entire process. If you are really looking to sell an aircraft and get the best possible price, having a professional do it can sometimes be a good option.

Selling It Yourself

Do you want to skip the broker and sell the aircraft yourself? This can be a perfectly viable option for someone who has the time and knows the market well enough to manage the process on their own. This is especially true in active buyer markets where listings are attacked by multiple buyers and because online advertising has become the norm for most buyers to browse to find aircraft they want to purchase. If you have an aircraft that you know will sell quickly, it may make sense to skip the use of a broker.

Good examples of aircraft of a specific make and model that are well maintained can often command a premium price and a quick sale. Be honest with yourself if your aircraft is really one that fits this description. If it is, list it in several places and see what happens.

If you choose to not use a broker initially, it doesn't mean you must finalize a sale that way. You may choose to test the market for a few weeks by listing the aircraft for sale and waiting to see if a quick sale develops. If not, you may choose to change your tactics later.

If you are planning to sell your aircraft on your own, make sure you or someone else will have the time and ability to respond to phone calls, emails, and requests to see the aircraft. If you work 70 hours a week or are gone for months at a time, have a family member or a fellow pilot friend help you when needed. Buyers will quickly move on to other options if you can't respond with requested information, return calls, or show the aircraft when appropriate.

Don't be afraid to list the aircraft for sale on multiple websites. Buyers will look at different sites, and having your aircraft listed on multiple ones will increase the chances that buyers will find your aircraft on the particular sites they choose to visit. You do not need to list your aircraft on each and every website you find, but it can be a good idea to select a few different sites.

Following are some of the top listing websites:

- AeroTrader—www.aerotrader.com
- Aircraft Dealer Network—www.findaircraft.com
- AirplaneMart (Facebook-based)—www.facebook.com/AirplaneMart
- AvBuyer—www.avbuyer.com
- Aircraft Shopper Online—www.aso.com
- Barnstormers—www.barnstormers.com
- Controller—www.controller.com
- Global Plane Search—www.globalplanesearch.com
- The Plane Exchange Network—www.theplaneexchange.com
- Trade-A-Plane—www.trade-a-plane.com

Each of these websites has strengths and weaknesses. Some of them focus more on business aircraft and the higher-end market, some focus on specialty aircraft such as experimental, seaplanes, or agricultural aircraft, and others just try to get as many general aviation listings as possible. These websites also vary in how much they charge for listing an aircraft. They will commonly charge more for listings that are extensive or that have a larger number of uploaded pictures.

It can also be a really good idea to share your aircraft listing on aircraft type club pages or social media groups. These often generate leads quickly and get shared between users who may know friends or others looking for specific types of aircraft. With the numerous internet resources now available, the spread of information happens much faster than ever before, and ensuring that your listing is visible and easily shared can make the difference between only a few or hundreds of potential buyers seeing your aircraft.

I don't encourage buyers to focus on print advertising of aircraft anymore. Sorry to those companies that still produce these, but in most cases, by the time a print listing is completed, the good aircraft have already been sold. This advice applies to sellers, as well. If you are paying for an online listing that includes accompanying print ads, then that's great; otherwise, don't spend the extra money.

Pricing Your Aircraft

Everyone wants to get top dollar for their aircraft. It's even better if you can make a profit on the sale! But that isn't the reality in many cases. If you bought an aircraft 10 years ago for $100,000 and have not completed any improvements, overhauled an engine, or redone the interior after 1,000 hours of flying it, don't expect that you'll be able to sell it for the same price. It's important to be realistic about what sale price you should expect the aircraft to command.

Complete a VREF valuation (www.vref.com) to get a good idea of the market value of your aircraft. If you happen to be an AOPA member, this service is free. VREF is basically the aircraft equivalent of the Kelley Blue Book for cars that many people are familiar with, and it should provide you with a "high market value" for your aircraft.

Once you have that information, spend time searching a few of the online listing sites I recommended previously as if you were a buyer. Compare and contrast aircraft currently for sale at various asking prices with the qualities of your aircraft. This will give you a baseline of what the market looks like in terms of asking prices for similar aircraft.

If you want to take your efforts to a higher level, get an aircraft appraisal done. An official appraisal may be desirable to help you determine an asking price, especially for premium aircraft. Visit the Professional Aircraft Appraisal Organization, LLC (PAAO) at www.appraiseaplane.org to find a certified aircraft appraiser if you want to take this additional step.

Once you have all this information, you can settle on an asking price. If the aircraft is a "premium" aircraft—that is, if it is extremely well kept, has fresh paint and interior, has a low-time engine, and really is the best the market has to offer—do not be shy about asking a premium price. If it doesn't fit this description, price it appropriately. If a buyer can buy a premium aircraft in a competitive market for $200,000 and you are asking $250,000, they will pass on your listing and you won't get many inquiries.

It may become difficult to price an aircraft in a case where you have put more into it than the market prices indicate it is worth. If your aircraft make and model is typically selling for $80,000 but you have recently paid for a $30,000 avionics upgrade, a $20,000 paint job, and a $40,000 engine overhaul on the aircraft, it may be a bitter pill to swallow. Even though your aircraft has $90,000 worth of upgrades, you may end up selling it for a $10,000 loss, not even counting the original asset acquisition costs. Unfortunately, that can sometimes be the cold, hard reality.

Never list your aircraft below comparable market prices unless you are willing to go lower than a competitive price and/or are clear about the price being non-negotiable. Aircraft buyers generally consider prices of aircraft to be negotiable and will try to bargain down the price. Plan ahead for these negotiations and leave yourself a little wiggle room in the price. This is typically true except in certain unique aircraft markets where an asking price may be considered firm due to scarcity of the aircraft make and model. If you are selling a rare, pristine Beechcraft Staggerwing that your estranged uncle George unexpectedly left you when he passed away, you can probably command a premium price without negotiation. But in most cases, be ready for a buyer to offer lower than list price.

In a general sense, I tell most buyers and sellers that if they settle on an aircraft's VREF price as the final sale price, the seller is getting a favorable deal. If the agreed-upon price is 80–90 percent of the VREF (or appraisal) price of the aircraft, both the buyer and seller are probably getting a fair deal. And if the final price is below 80 percent of the market price for the aircraft, the buyer is getting a good deal. If it's lower than 70 percent, it's a *great* deal for the buyer, and the seller should consider a sale at prices that low to be "motivated." In some cases, these can be considered sales of "distress" by an owner who just really needs or wants to get rid of the aircraft.

In the end, it is a negotiation. A buyer may try to get a discount for any discrepancies on the aircraft while a seller will try to play up its positive attributes. When you are selling your aircraft, keep in mind that you don't have to sell to the first person who makes an offer. There will be other buyers. If the offer is fair and agreeable, accept it. If not, take the buyer's contact information and say you will consider the offer.

Tips to Make Your Aircraft More Saleable

If you're trying to sell your aircraft, you want to get buyers interested and eager to buy. It is amazing how many times I have seen bad listings, terrible planning, or lazy owners cause potential buyers to hesitate to inquire about an aircraft or just walk away because of things that would have been very simple to address.

Based on my many experiences buying and selling planes and helping others through this process, I have discovered a few simple tips that may help you attract more interested buyers and sell your aircraft more quickly and at a higher price.

Clean the aircraft.

A dirty aircraft is the issue that is most commonly overlooked and simplest to address but that I see far too many sellers ignore. If your aircraft has been sitting in a dirty hangar for months, it is going to look derelict. Clean it inside and out. Wash it, polish it, clean the windows, vacuum the interior, clean the leather or vinyl, and even clean the side walls and headliner fabric. A dirty plane looks like it has not been cared for by its owner.

Don't forget to get under the belly. Exhaust and oil residue can make it look bad and may give the impression that a problem exists. Every airplane has some oil and dirt residue on its belly, but if it hasn't been cleaned for 10 years, it could make it look like something more serious.

Do the work to clean the aircraft well—inside, outside, and underneath.

Clean mechanical items.
A clean engine area looks like it is being carefully maintained. De-cowl the aircraft and get in there with rags and mineral spirits to clean under the cowling. Wipe down oily areas of the cowling, engine, or other components. Don't forget to wipe off the back of constant-speed propellers. A tiny seep of oil from a prop seal can look like a big leak if the oil is left there over time rather than being cleaned off. Honestly, this is also good advice for any owner keeping an aircraft, because if you don't clean these items regularly, it won't be as easy to notice any new leak problems that are developing. Take the time to make the mechanical components look clean so buyers will understand that any problems would not easily go unnoticed.

Fix or replace simple plastic parts such as fairings.
Wing root fairings, wing or stabilator tips, and other simple plastic parts wear and break faster than most other items on an aircraft, and if these are not fixed, they may make the aircraft show poorly. For a few hundred dollars, many of these can be replaced quickly and easily, and in some cases this work can even be legally done by owners themselves if they are mechanically inclined. A little investment in these parts can eliminate cosmetic issues on the outside of the aircraft and will raise far fewer questions about its mechanical soundness. If nothing else, even a savvy buyer who understands the minimal airworthiness effect of many of these parts may be more likely to buy an aircraft if they don't see a "bunch of little things" they will need to address after the purchase.

Adding seat covers is a great way to spruce up (and cover) worn seats.
In many planes, the front two seats take the bulk of the beating. They may look much more worn than back seats and as a result, show poorly. You could go through the effort of reupholstering the seats, or you could much more easily just put good seat

covers on them. For a few hundred dollars, sheepskin seat covers are available for many aircraft makes and models. This can be quicker and cheaper than having seats reupholstered, and as a side benefit, the covers often more comfortable and cooler than the original upholstery! Offering seat covers with the aircraft can be a selling benefit to offer buyers and will cover worn seats that might otherwise detract from how well the aircraft shows.

Replace simple interior cosmetic items.
Worn and unreadable panel placards, broken pieces on yokes, and cracked or broken air vents can often be replaced for a minimal cost. Some of these replacements must be completed by a mechanic, but this can easily be worked into an annual inspection process as you prepare an aircraft to be sold. It's worth taking the time to fix these items on your aircraft if they are broken. Although you may have gotten used to just "living with" these simple, broken parts, they make the aircraft look bad to a potential buyer. Do not disregard them when you are trying to sell the aircraft, as many buyers won't be willing to "live with" these types of minor broken items.

Repaint wing walk.
On low-wing aircraft, or even on the steps of high-wing aircraft, wing walk gets faded and looks worn or dated. Many aircraft parts suppliers or pilot supply shops offer small cans of wing walk paint that anyone can buy. With a little masking tape and a paintbrush, you can quickly freshen up those wing walk areas. A fresh, dark black, gritty wing walk is a simple way to spruce up the aircraft.

Remove the clutter of handheld devices.
I know you may love your 15-year-old handheld GPS that you stuck to the yoke on a temporary mount, but the next buyer may not want it, may have more current equipment, or may simply like a decluttered cockpit. Therefore, it's best just to remove it. I recommend removing any non-permanent, handheld, or temporarily attached wires and gadgets in the cockpit. Of course, any items that you'll be including in the sale, such as a new, modern, handheld GPS unit, should be included in the listing notes. I encourage included items to be available for viewing, but not necessarily in the

aircraft when you show it or in pictures. These can make aircraft cabins and cockpits look cluttered. A jumble of wires will look more like a hazard to entry and exit of the aircraft than a real benefit for any actual pilot use. You don't want a buyer to feel like they will need to crawl through a bird's nest to get into the pilot seat.

Take good pictures.
Now that you have taken the time to fix a bunch of mostly cosmetic concerns, it's time to take photos. Any buyer who isn't close enough to drop in and look at the aircraft for a first look will start their buying effort by looking at the pictures you provide. Don't provide junk.

Pictures taken in dark hangars, in the rain on a cloudy day, or with a bad phone camera do not show an aircraft well. Many phones have great cameras on them nowadays and can take great photos if used properly. Using either a quality camera or phone camera, take the time to get really good photos of the aircraft in favorable lighting, preferably outside on a sunny day. It doesn't hurt to get a few pictures in really cool places (like a nice sod strip for a backcountry aircraft or an island with the ocean in the background for a good traveling aircraft) to help would-be buyers imagine how and where they could use that aircraft they are going to buy!

Make sure you have pictures of everything, and do not omit pictures as a way to hide things you don't want a buyer to see. Take photos of the panel, the interior (front and back seats), baggage areas, the engine with the cowling off, inside the tail, the floor, wings, wing tips, wheel pants (if available), etc. I think you see the point—take lots of pictures. A buyer who sees many pictures will think the seller is serious about providing a true representation of the aircraft.

Although it probably should go without saying, too many sellers don't heed this advice: Make sure to take these photographs after—not before—you have cleaned and prettied up the aircraft. These pictures are the first impression buyers will get of your aircraft during the sale process. Make an effort to ensure this first impression is positive and effective.

Have good copies of your logbooks available (in digital format, if possible).

Most buyers will want to see aircraft logbooks and supplemental information before they finalize a purchase. Have these available, organized, and clearly understandable. If you hand a potential buyer a box of jumbled papers, it may give the impression that the maintenance of the aircraft has not been very well-managed and organized.

Take the time to organize engine, aircraft, and propeller logs if you haven't already done so. Make sure current airworthiness directive (AD) and service bulletin (SB) (if applicable) tracking logs are available to show that these requirements have been complied with.

It can be a great idea to make these available digitally. Scanning your aircraft's logbooks and saving them in PDF format will allow you to more easily send them to potential buyers for review and provide information many buyers will want to see. Don't worry, you do not need a big, fancy scanner to get this done. There are great scanning applications available for most phones and digital tablets that will allow you to take a picture and convert it to a PDF. I create digital copies of the logbooks and supporting information for every aircraft I own. This is also a great way to ensure you have a backup copy of your logbooks in case they ever are damaged or lost.

Carefully consider any upgrades for sale purposes.

Do you want to spend a little more time or money to make your aircraft more saleable? Below are some additional tips that cost a little more but that might be worth considering if you are planning to sell your aircraft a little further out in the future.

Most of the time, upgrading an aircraft prior to sale will not generate a full return on the investment made. Therefore, if you are looking to sell your aircraft soon, my advice is typically to not spend any money on upgrades. But, if you are looking at selling the aircraft at a future point in time and are considering upgrades that you would use in the interim, take into account what upgrades would make the aircraft more palatable to buyers when you go to sell.

Remove broken or inoperative avionics equipment from the panel.

This is the first change that I always recommend to owners who are going to sell an aircraft—and honestly, even for owners who plan to keep their aircraft. A buyer looking at a panel full of broken instruments or avionics will get a negative impression of the overall condition of the aircraft. Have that old rotary DME or LORAN removed and cover their places in the panel with a clean blank spot. It is better to have less equipment and a streamlined, fully functioning, clean panel than it is to have a bunch of avionics that don't work. Broken equipment takes up space and makes a panel look junky.

Remember to have the weight and balance updated, too—for example, if you remove an old, 35-pound ADF that hasn't worked for two decades. It is surprising how much the weight can be affected when removing older equipment from the panel. I rarely recommend that sellers go to the trouble of having all the wiring removed at the same time as the equipment, although this is up to you. That wiring is not what the next owner will see on a first impression, but they will see the clean panel when you remove the inoperative equipment. Most buyers won't think to look through the airplane for unused wiring left over from previously removed avionics equipment.

A great time to have broken equipment removed is during the aircraft's annual inspection. A fresh annual can help sell an aircraft, so take the time to have broken equipment removed when you get that last pre-sale annual completed.

Upgrade avionics that make the aircraft more useful.

There are times in the aviation industry when certain features will make aircraft more desirable. This occurred when Mode C transponders became a requirement in many airspaces, when GPS systems became common in general aviation aircraft, and when ADS-B became a desirable "upgrade" due to future regulation changes. If you are trying to sell an aircraft that does not have these features, it may be harder to find a buyer. Upgrading avionics can be expensive, but if you plan to keep your aircraft for a few years before selling, it may be worth doing for your own personal use and to enhance resale value at a future date. Keep an eye on what features a typical buyer will likely be seeking when you plan to sell. Your options will be to either provide what buyers are looking for or discount your price to a point where it will be competitive in the market after taking into account the buyer's expense to install those features after purchase.

Paint the cowling.

A cracked and rough-looking cowling can quickly detract from the overall appearance of an aircraft. The cowling is also what takes the biggest beating and is often the first thing to start looking worn or develop cracked paint. The good news is that on many aircraft, it is the easiest thing to remove and have a fresh paint job completed on. For a minimal cost, removing the cowling and having it stripped and freshly painted can quickly improve the overall appearance of the aircraft.

Paint the aircraft.

If the paint on your aircraft is really rough, it might make sense to get a fresh paint job on the entire aircraft. Painting an aircraft isn't cheap, but it can make a big difference in sales efforts. Let's be honest, shiny and new-looking aircraft are easier to sell. A savvy buyer will probably be more focused on mechanical soundness of the aircraft, but as much as I hate to admit it, most buyers aren't as savvy as we might wish. Shop carefully, be willing to fly the aircraft somewhere for a paint job, and carefully evaluate the market so you know what the going sales prices are for your aircraft. Then you can consider if the investment of a paint job will generate enough increase in a sales price to make it worth it.

Overhaul the propeller.

Like engines, propellers—especially those that are constant speed—also get overhauls. A high-time propeller, leaking prop hub, or chipped and nicked propeller blades can dissuade a potential buyer from moving forward. These things can become airworthiness issues. But even if the airworthiness is not compromised, it might be worth overhauling a propeller before trying to sell an aircraft.

A pro tip if you do this: Make sure the logbooks detail why the propeller was overhauled. A propeller overhaul taking place out of sync with an engine overhaul can often make mechanics and potential buyers question why it was done. If it was a leaking hub, make sure that is noted. If it was because the prop had some nicks in it from gravel, indicate the propeller was overhauled due to nicks in the blade. Leaving this blank in the logbook can result in buyers wondering if there was a propeller strike that didn't include an engine inspection or overhaul.

Overhaul the engine.
Aircraft with high-time engines can sometimes be hard to sell. Buyers who are focused on "manufacturer's recommended overhaul" times may avoid buying an aircraft with a high-time engine, thus limiting your potential sales market. If you are planning ahead for a sale, you could get an engine overhaul done and fly the aircraft another couple years, perhaps for 300–400 hours, and then sell it with a low-time engine. It will command a better sales price. I don't believe I have ever seen a freshly overhauled engine command enough of an increase in sales price to counterbalance the cost of removing, overhauling, and reinstalling the engine, but it may be worth doing so if you're finding the aircraft hard to sell or if you are planning ahead to make a future sale more successful. Shop carefully for an engine overhaul if you decide to do it. Shops vary in the quality of the work they do, but when it comes time to sell the aircraft, the sale price you can get will probably only vary minimally based on which shop did the overhaul.

Be honest about any shortcomings of the aircraft.
Buyers do not want to be surprised with any problems in an aircraft they are considering buying. Therefore, don't surprise them. This doesn't mean you must point out every little nick or scratch, but don't try to hide things that are actually wrong. A buyer's pre-buy inspection or even a thorough walk around the aircraft will quickly show them any issues that you didn't bother to tell them about or that you hid in pictures.

If the seats are torn up, show this in a picture and tell the buyer. Reflect it in the price and move on from there. If the paint is worn and 30 years old, don't list its condition as a 9 out of 10 and just hope the buyer does not notice later. They will.

Most buyers will go much further into the process when they're dealing with an honest broker or seller who is telling them all the details than with one who seems like a used car salesman trying to sell them a lemon.

. . .

Many of these recommendations may sound like an effort to "pretty up the pig" for sale, but they can really make a difference to potential buyers and are often very easy for a seller to do.

Real estate agents are masters of staging houses they are trying to sell in order to show them in a favorable light to potential buyers. Why shouldn't a broker or aircraft owner do the same thing when trying to sell an aircraft? This doesn't mean you should hide known discrepancies in the aircraft or its airworthiness, but it does mean you should show your aircraft to a potential buyer in the best possible condition.

When the aircraft is being shown in person, ensure there is good lighting in the hangar or have the aircraft outside and shown during daylight. A dark, dingy hangar will not show the aircraft in the best possible light—both literally and figuratively. Although it might not seem important, if you have a poorly lit hangar, be sure to show the aircraft outside or set up some shop lights.

Take the time to "stage" your aircraft and make it look as good as possible. Don't let a would-be buyer get turned off because of simple things which could have been easily addressed and that detract from the aircraft showing well.

Negotiating and Finalizing the Sale

When a buyer is ready to move forward with a purchase, you may have some additional work and decisions to make. Following are important considerations and recommendations to help you through this stage.

Allowing a Pre-Buy Inspection

Many buyers will request some sort of pre-buy inspection be completed on the aircraft. I advise most buyers I work with to have a pre-buy inspection completed by a maintenance technician other than the one who normally does the maintenance on the aircraft. This prevents interested parties from being the determining factor in documenting any discrepancies on an aircraft. With that in mind, a pre-buy inspection will typically be completed by a maintenance technician who is working for the buyer, not the seller. It can be a good idea for the seller to be present during this pre-buy inspection to demand that anyone taking the aircraft apart be a reputable maintenance provider who is familiar with the make and model of aircraft. Another option would be to have the seller's maintenance provider present in place of the seller themselves. The provider may also be able to offer answers, based on knowledge of the aircraft's historical maintenance record, to any questions the maintenance technician might have during completion of the inspection.

Conducting Test Flights

Frequently, pilots or representatives of theirs will want to test fly an aircraft prior to purchase. This can be part of the pre-buy inspection process, helping the buyer determine if there are any equipment items that need maintenance or discrepancies that can't be found only with a ground inspection. However, I never encourage a seller to just hand the keys over to a random pilot from four states away who says, "I might want to buy your plane."

A seller should conduct a demonstration flight or have a properly qualified pilot of their choosing do this. It may be possible to allow an instructor to fly with a potential buyer to demonstrate the aircraft. No matter who is flying the aircraft, make sure you have considered whether insurance coverage will apply and, if not, whether you are willing to take that risk.

Finalizing a Price

At some point, the buyer is going to make an offer, and it may or may not be the asking price you started with. If the buyer had a pre-buy inspection completed that identified concerns, you may be left with the choice of either discounting the needed work from the asking price or fixing the items at your own cost. You may choose to negotiate delivery of the aircraft or ask the buyer to pick it up where it is hangared. No matter what discussion develops, it is likely that the buyer will ask for a slightly lower price. In some cases, this goes the other way. I have seen active buying markets in which sought-after aircraft attract multiple offers and prices are actually bid up beyond asking prices. Kudos if you find this happening to you. On the other hand, perhaps it means you priced the aircraft too low in the first place.

The sale price you agree to in the end really becomes a personal and situational decision. It may be dependent on factors such as whether you have an outstanding loan on the aircraft, if you have a misplaced expectation of greater-than-market value of the aircraft, or if you just really are not ready to sell and are unwilling to accept a lower price. Be sure to consider all the factors as you determine if a buyer is offering a fair and acceptable price.

If you do agree on a price with a buyer, it will then be time to complete some paperwork.

Doing the Paperwork

Never ever let your aircraft leave your control until payment has cleared and all transfer documents have been completed. Although it's not overly common, some scams do occur. More importantly, a deposit is not full payment. You don't want to find yourself in a situation where your aircraft is already halfway across the country when the buyer's check bounces or the expected wire transfer doesn't come through. The old adage "possession is nine-tenths of the law" kind of applies here. Getting your aircraft back could at a minimum be a logistical challenge in a failed sale process.

Complete all bills of sale, monetary transference, or closings while you are still in control of the aircraft. This doesn't necessarily mean that the aircraft must remain at your home airport; you could choose to deliver the aircraft to another location, but the registration and keys should not go to the new owner until all paperwork and payments are done. In many transfers of ownership, an escrow service may be a good option.

If you do not have experience with the aircraft sale process, ask for help. Find a local instructor or broker who has regularly helped others with the process of transferring aircraft ownership. Even if you are not using a broker for the sale, many brokers will be willing, for a nominal fee, to help a buyer and seller get the paperwork done by showing up at a scheduled closing. It can be well worth a few dollars to make sure the paperwork that is submitted does not end up coming back from the FAA because it is incorrect or incomplete.

• • •

Selling your aircraft can be tough and it takes some work, but with a little forethought, it can result in a fair sales price for you. Regardless of the reason, if you ever decide to sell your aircraft, these tips can help make the process smooth and assist you in getting the best possible sales price.

About the Author

Jason Blair is an active instructor and FAA-designated pilot examiner who has worked for many years in the aviation training industry. He has flown and instructed in more than 100 makes and models of general aviation aircraft and through his experience has learned enough to share some knowledge that may be useful to others. He writes for multiple aviation publications and has worked for and with aviation associations and the FAA as an industry representative within the general aviation community. He has also owned numerous general aviation aircraft for both business and personal use and admits he will no doubt own more aircraft in the future. To learn more about Jason Blair and his industry involvement, visit www.JasonBlair.net.